The English Gipsies and Their Language

Charles G. Leland

I0118709

Contents

THE ENGLISH GIPSIES
AND THEIR LANGUAGE

BY

Charles G. Leland

PREFACE.

As Author of this book, I beg leave to observe that all which is stated in it relative to the customs or peculiarities of Gipsies *was gathered directly from Gipsies themselves*; and that every word of their language here given, whether in conversations, stories, or sayings, was taken from Gipsy mouths. While entertaining the highest respect for the labours of Mr George Borrow in this field, I have carefully avoided repeating him in the least detail; neither have I taken anything from Simson, Hoyland, or any other writer on the Rommany race in England. Whatever the demerits of the work may be, it can at least claim to be an original collection of material fresh from nature, and not a reproduction from books. There are, it is true, two German Gipsy letters from other works, but these may be excused as illustrative of an English one.

I may here in all sincerity speak kindly and gratefully of every true Gipsy I have ever met, and of the cheerfulness with which they have invariably assisted me in my labour to the extent of their humble abilities. Other writers have had much to say of their incredible distrust of *Gorgios* and unwillingness to impart their language, but I have always found them obliging and communicative. I have never had occasion to complain of rapacity or greediness among them; on the contrary, I have often wondered to see how the great want of such very poor people was generally kept in check by their natural politeness, which always manifests itself when they are treated properly. In fact, the first effort which I ever made to acquire a knowledge of English Rommany originated in a voluntary offer from an intelligent old dame to teach me "the old Egyptian language." And as she also suggested that I should set forth the knowledge which I might acquire from her and her relatives in a book (referring to Mr Borrow's having done so), I may hold myself fully acquitted from the charge of having acquired and published anything which my Gipsy friends would not have had made known to the public.

Mr Borrow has very well and truly said that it is not by passing a few hours among Gipsies that one can acquire a knowledge of their characteristics; and I think that this book presents abundant evidence that its contents were not gathered by slight and superficial intercourse with the Rommany. It is only by entering gradually and sympathetically, without any parade of patronage, into a familiar knowledge of the circumstances of the common life of humble people, be they Gipsies, Indians, or whites, that one can surprise unawares those little inner traits which constitute the ***characteristic***. However this may be, the reader will readily enough understand, on perusing these pages--possibly much better than I do myself--how it was I was able to collect whatever they contain that is new.

The book contains some remarks on that great curious centre and secret of all the nomadic and vagabond life in England, THE ROMMANY, with comments on the fact, that of the many novel or story-writers who 'have described the "Travellers" of the Roads, very few have penetrated the real nature of their life. It gives several incidents illustrating the character of the Gipsy, and some information of a very curious nature in reference to the respect of the English Gipsies for their dead, and the strange manner in which they testify it. I believe that this will be found to be fully and distinctly illustrated by anecdotes and a narrative in the original Gipsy language, with a translation. There is also a chapter containing in Rommany and English a very characteristic letter from a full-blood Gipsy to a relative, which was dictated to me, and which gives a sketch of the leading incidents of Gipsy life--trading in horses, fortune-telling, and cock-shying. I have also given accounts of conversations with Gipsies, introducing in their language and in English their own remarks (noted down by me) on certain curious customs; among others, on one which indicates that many of them profess among themselves a certain regard for our Saviour, because His birth and life appear to them to be like that of the Rommany. There is a collection of a number of words now current in vulgar English which were probably derived from Gipsy, such as row, shindy, pal, trash, bosh, and niggling, and finally a number of ***Gudli*** or short stories. These ***Gudli*** have been regarded by my literary friends as interesting and curious, since they are nearly all specimens of a form of original narrative occupying a middle ground between the anecdote and fable, and abounding in Gipsy traits. Some of them are given word for word as they are current among Gipsies, and others owe their existence almost entirely either to the vivid imagination and childlike fancies of an old Gipsy assistant, or were developed from some hint or imperfect saying or story. But all are thoroughly and truly Rommany; for every one, after being brought into shape, passed through a purely "unsophisticated" Gipsy mind, and was finally declared to be *tacho*, or sound, by real Rommanis. The truth is, that it is a difficult matter to hear a story among English Gipsies which is not mangled or marred in the telling; so that to print it, restitution and invention become inevitable. But with a man who lived in a tent among the gorse and fern, and who intermitted his earnest conversation with a little wooden bear to point out to me the gentleman on horseback riding over the two beautiful little girls in the flowers on the carpet, such fables as I have given sprang up of themselves, owing nothing to books, though they often required the influence of a better disciplined mind to guide them to a consistent termination.

The Rommany English Vocabulary which I propose shall follow this work is many times over more extensive than any ever before published, and it will also be found interesting to all philologists by its establishing the very curious fact that this last wave of the primitive Aryan-Indian ocean which spread over Europe, though it has lost the original form in its subsidence and degradation, consists of the same substance--or, in other words, that although the grammar has wellnigh disappeared, the words are almost without exception the same as those used in India, Germany, Hungary, or Turkey. It is generally believed that English Gipsy is a mere jargon of the cant and slang of all nations, that of England predominating; but a very slight examination of the Vocabulary will show that during more than three hundred years in England the Rommany have not admitted a single English word to what they correctly call their language. I mean, of course, so far as my own knowledge of Rommany extends. To this at least I can testify, that the Gipsy to whom I was principally indebted for words, though he often used "slang," invariably discriminated correctly between it and Rommany; and I have often admired the extraordinary pride in their language which has induced the Gipsies for so many generations to teach their children this difference. {0a} Almost every word which my assistant declared to be Gipsy I have found either in Hindustani or in the works of Pott, Liebich, or Paspati. On this subject I would remark by the way, that many words which appear to have been taken by the Gipsies from modern languages are in reality Indian.

And as I have honestly done what I could to give the English reader fresh material on the Gipsies, and not a rewarming of that which was gathered by others, I sincerely trust that I may not be held to sharp account (as the authors of such books very often are) for not having given more or done more or done it better than was really in my power. Gipsies in England are passing away as rapidly as Indians in North America. They keep among themselves the most singular fragments of their Oriental origin; they abound in quaint characteristics, and yet almost nothing is done to preserve what another generation will deeply regret the loss of. There are complete dictionaries of the Dacotah and many other American Indian languages, and every detail of the rude life of those savages has been carefully recorded; while the autobiographic romances of Mr Borrow and Mr Simson's History contain nearly all the information of any value extant relative to the English Gipsies. Yet of these two writers, Mr Borrow is the only one who had, so to speak, an inside view of his subject, or was a philologist.

In conclusion I would remark, that if I have not, like many writers on the poor Gipsies, abused them for certain proverbial faults, it has been because they never troubled me with anything very serious of the kind, or brought it to my notice; and I certainly never took the pains to hunt it up to the discredit of people who always behaved decently to me. I have found them more cheerful, polite, and grateful than the lower orders of other races in Europe or America; and I believe that where their respect and sympathy are secured, they are quite as upright. Like all people who are regarded as outcasts, they are very proud of being trusted, and under this influence will commit the most daring acts of honesty. And with this I commend my book to the public. Should it be favourably received, I will add fresh reading to it; in any case I shall at least have the satisfaction of knowing that I did my best to collect material illustrating a very curious and greatly-neglected subject. It is merely as a collection of material that I offer it; let those who can use it, do what they will with it.

If I have not given in this book a sketch of the history of the Gipsies, or statistics of their numbers, or accounts of their social condition in different countries, it is because nearly everything of the kind may be found in the works of George Borrow and Walter Simson, which are in all respectable libraries, and may be obtained from any bookseller.

I would remark to any impatient reader for mere entertainment, who may find fault with the abundance of Rommany or Gipsy language in the following pages, that ***the principal object of the Author was to collect and preserve such specimens of a rapidly-vanishing language***, and that the title-page itself indirectly indicates such an object. I have, however, invariably given with the Gipsy a translation immediately following the text in plain English--at times very plain--in order that the literal meaning of words may be readily apprehended. I call especial attention to this fact, so that no one may accuse me of encumbering my pages with Rommany.

While writing this book, or in fact after the whole of the first part was written, I passed a winter in Egypt; and as that country is still supposed by many people to be the fatherland of the Gipsies, and as very little is known relative to the Rommany there, I have taken the liberty of communicating what I could learn on the subject, though it does not refer directly to the Gipsies of England. Those who are interested in the latter will readily pardon the addition.

There are now in existence about three hundred works on the Gipsies, but of the entire number comparatively few contain fresh material gathered from the Rommany themselves. Of late years the first philologists of Europe have taken a great interest in their language, which is now included in "Die Sprachen Europas" as the only Indian tongue spoken in this quarter of the world; and I believe that English Gipsy is really the only strongly-distinct Rommany dialect which has never as yet been illustrated by copious specimens or a vocabulary of any extent. I therefore trust that the critical reader will make due allowances for the very great difficulties under which I have laboured, and not blame me for not having done better that which, so far as I can ascertain, would possibly not have been done at all. Within the memory of man the popular Rommany of this country was really grammatical; that which is now spoken, and from which I gathered the material for the following pages, is, as the reader will observe, almost entirely English as to its structure, although it still abounds in Hindu words to a far greater extent than has been hitherto supposed.

CHAPTER I. INTRODUCTORY.

The Rommany of the Roads.--The Secret of Vagabond Life in England.--Its peculiar and thoroughly hidden Nature.--Gipsy Character and the Causes which formed it.--Moral Results of hungry Marauding.--Gipsy ideas of Religion. The Scripture story of the Seven Whistlers.--The Baker's Daughter.--Difficulties of acquiring Rommany.--The Fable of the Cat.--The Chinese, the American Indian, and the Wandering Gipsy.

Although the valuable and curious works of Mr George Borrow have been in part for more than twenty years before the British public, {1} it may still be doubted whether many, even of our scholars, are aware of the remarkable, social, and philological facts which are connected with an immense proportion of our out-of-door population. There are, indeed, very few people who know, that every time we look from the window into a crowded street, the chances are greatly in favour of the assertion, that we shall see at least one man who bears in his memory some hundreds of Sanscrit roots, and that man English born; though it was probably in the open air, and English bred, albeit his breeding was of the roads.

For go where you will, though you may not know it, you encounter at every step, in one form or the other, *the Rommany*. True, the dwellers in tents are becoming few and far between, because the "close cultivation" of the present generation, which has enclosed nearly all the waste land in England, has left no spot in many a day's journey, where "the travellers," as they call themselves, can light the fire and boil the kettle undisturbed. There is almost "no tan to hatch," or place to stay in. So it has come to pass, that those among them who cannot settle down like unto the Gentiles, have gone across the Great Water to America, which is their true Canaan, where they flourish mightily, the more enterprising making a good thing of it, by ***prastering graias*** or "running horses," or trading in them, while the idler or more moral ones, pick up their living as easily as a mouse in a cheese, on the endless roads and in the forests.   And so many of them have gone there, that I am sure the child is now born, to whom the sight of a real old-fashioned gipsy will be as rare in England as a Sioux or Pawnee warrior in the streets of New York or Philadelphia.   But there is a modified and yet real Rommany-dom, which lives and will live with great vigour, so long as a regularly organised nomadic class exists on our roads--and it is the true nature and inner life of this class which has remained for ages, an impenetrable mystery to the world at large.   A member of it may be a tramp and a beggar, the proprietor of some valuable travelling show, a horse-dealer, or a tinker.   He may be eloquent, as a Cheap Jack, noisy as a Punch, or musical with a fiddle at fairs.   He may "peddle" pottery, make and sell skewers and clothes-pegs, or vend baskets in a caravan; he may keep cock-shys and Aunt Sallys at races.   But whatever he may be, depend upon it, reader, that among those who follow these and similar callings which he represents, are literally many thousands who, unsuspected by the ***Gorgios***, are known to one another, and who still speak among themselves, more or less, that curious old tongue which the researches of the greatest living philologists have indicated, is in all probability not merely allied to Sanscrit, but perhaps in point of age, an elder though vagabond sister or cousin of that ancient language.

For THE ROMMANY is the characteristic leaven of all the real tramp life and nomadic callings of Great Britain.   And by this word I mean not the language alone, which is regarded, however, as a test of superior knowledge of "the roads," but a curious ***inner life*** and freemasonry of secret intelligence, ties of blood and information, useful to a class who have much in common with one another, and very little in common with the settled tradesman or worthy citizen.   The hawker whom you meet, and whose blue eyes and light hair indicate no trace of Oriental blood, may not be a ***churdo***, or ***pash-ratt***, or half-blood, or ***half-scrag***, as a full Gipsy might contemptuously term him, but he may be, of his kind, a quadroon or octoroon, or he may have "gipsified," by marrying a Gipsy wife; and by the way be it said, such women make by far the best wives to be found among English itinerants, and the best suited for "a traveller." But in any case he has taken pains to pick up all the Gipsy he can.   If he is a tinker, he knows ***Kennick***, or cant, or thieves' slang by nature, but the Rommany, which has very few words in common with the former, is the true language of the mysteries; in fact, it has with him become, strangely enough, what it was originally, a sort of sacred Sanscrit, known only to the Brahmins of the roads, compared to which the other language is only commonplace *Prakrit*, which anybody may acquire.

He is proud of his knowledge, he makes of it a deep mystery; and if you, a gentleman, ask him about it, he will probably deny that he ever heard of its existence. Should he be very thirsty, and your manners frank and assuring, it is, however, not impossible that after draining a pot of beer at your expense, he may recall, with a grin, the fact that he *has* heard that the Gipsies have a queer kind of language of their own; and then, if you have any Rommany yourself at command, he will perhaps *rakker Rommanis* with greater or less fluency. Mr Simeon, in his "History of the Gipsies," asserts that there is not a tinker or scissors- grinder in Great Britain who cannot talk this language, and my own experience agrees with his declaration, to this extent--that they all have some knowledge of it, or claim to have it, however slight it may be.

So rare is a knowledge of Rommany among those who are not connected in some way with Gipsies, that the slightest indication of it is invariably taken as an irrefutable proof of relationship with them. It is but a few weeks since, as I was walking along the Marine Parade in Brighton, I overtook a tinker. Wishing him to sharpen some tools for me, I directed him to proceed to my home, and *en route* spoke to him in Gipsy. As he was quite fair in complexion, I casually remarked, "I should have never supposed you could speak Rommany--you don't look like it." To which he replied, very gravely, in a tone as of gentle reproach, "You don't look a Gipsy yourself, sir; but you know you *are* one-- *you talk like one*."

Truly, the secret of the Rommany has been well kept in England. It seems so to me when I reflect that, with the exception of Lavengro and the Rommany Rye, {5} I cannot recall a single novel, in our language, in which the writer has shown familiarity with the *real* life, habits, or language of the vast majority of that very large class, the itinerants of the roads. Mr Dickens has set before us Cheap Jacks, and a number of men who were, in their very face, of the class of which I speak; but I cannot recall in his writings any indication that he knew that these men had a singular secret life with their *confreres*, or that they could speak a strange language; for we may well call that language strange which is, in the main, Sanscrit, with many Persian words intermingled. Mr Dickens, however, did not pretend, as some have done, to specially treat of Gipsies, and he made no affectation of a knowledge of any mysteries. He simply reflected popular life as he saw it. But there are many novels and tales, old and new, devoted to setting forth Rommany life and conversation, which are as much like the originals as a Pastor Fido is like a common shepherd. One novel which I once read, is so full of "the dark blood," that it might almost be called a gipsy novel. The hero is a gipsy; he lives among his kind--the book is full of them; and yet, with all due respect to its author, who is one of the most gifted and best- informed romance writers of the century, I must declare that, from beginning to end, there is not in the novel the slightest indication of any real and familiar knowledge of gipsies. Again, to put thieves' slang into the mouths of gipsies, as their natural and habitual language, has been so much the custom, from Sir Walter Scott to the present day, that readers are sometimes gravely assured in good faith that this jargon is pure Rommany. But this is an old error in England, since the vocabulary of cant appended to the "English Rogue," published in 1680, was long believed to be Gipsy; and Captain Grose, the antiquary, who should have known better, speaks with the same ignorance.

It is, indeed, strange to see learned and shrewd writers, who pride themselves on truthfully depicting every element of European life, and every type of every society, so ignorant of the habits, manners, and language of thousands of really strange people who swarm on the highways and bye-ways! We have had the squire and the governess, my lord and all Bohemia--Bohemia, artistic and literary--but where are our *Vrais Bohemiens*?--Out of Lavengro and Rommany Rye--nowhere. Yet there is to be found among the children of Rom, or the descendants of the worshippers of Rama, or the Doms or Coptic Romi, whatever their ancestors may have been, more that is quaint and adapted to the purposes of the novelist, than is to be found in any other class of the inhabitants of England. You may not detect a trace of it on the roads; but once become truly acquainted with a fair average specimen of a Gipsy, pass many days in conversation with him, and above all acquire his confidence and respect, and you will wonder that such a being, so entirely different from yourself, could exist in Europe in the nineteenth century. It is said that those who can converse with Irish peasants in their own native tongue, form far higher opinions of their appreciation of the beautiful, and of the elements of humour and pathos in their hearts, than do those who know their thoughts only through the medium of English. I know from my own observation that this is quite the case with the Indians of North America, and it is unquestionably so with the Gipsy. When you know a true specimen to the depths of his soul, you will find a character so entirely strange, so utterly at variance with your ordinary conceptions of humanity, that it is no exaggeration whatever to declare that it would be a very difficult task for the best writer to convey to the most intelligent reader an idea of his subject's nature. You have in him, to begin with, a being whose every condition of life is in direct contradiction to what you suppose every man's life in England must be. "I was born in the open air," said a Gipsy to me a few days since; "and put me down anywhere, in the fields or woods, I can always support myself." Understand me, he did not mean by pilfering, since it was of America that we were speaking, and of living in the lonely forests. We pity with tears many of the poor among us, whose life is one of luxury compared to that which the Gipsy, who despises them, enjoys with a zest worth more than riches.

"What a country America must be," quoth Pirengro, the Walker, to me, on the occasion just referred to. "Why, my pal, who's just welled apopli from dovo tem-- (my brother, who has just returned from that country), tells me that when a cow or anything dies there, they just chuck it away, and nobody ask a word for any of it." "What would *you* do," he continued, "if you were in the fields and had nothing to eat?"

I replied, "that if any could be found, I should hunt for fern-roots."

"I could do better than that," he said. "I should hunt for a ***hotchewitchi***,--a hedge-hog,--and I should be sure to find one; there's no better eating."

Whereupon assuming his left hand to be an imaginary hedge-hog, he proceeded to score and turn and dress it for ideal cooking with a case-knife.

"And what had you for dinner to-day?" I inquired.

"Some cocks' heads. They're very fine--very fine indeed!"

Now it is curious but true that there is no person in the world more particular as to what he eats than the half-starved English or Irish peasant, whose sufferings have so often been set forth for our condolence. We may be equally foolish, you and I--in fact chemistry proves it--when we are disgusted at the idea of feeding on many things which mere association and superstition render revolting. But the old fashioned gipsy has none of these qualms--he is haunted by no ghost of society--save the policeman, he knows none of its terrors. Whatever is edible he eats, except horse-meat; wherever there is an empty spot he sleeps; and the man who can do this devoid of shame, without caring a pin for what the world says--nay, without even knowing that he does not care, or that he is peculiar--is independent to a degree which of itself confers a character which is not easy to understand.

I grew up as a young man with great contempt for Helvetius, D'Holbach, and all the French philosophers of the last century, whose ideal man was a perfect savage; but I must confess that since I have studied gipsy nature, my contempt has changed into wonder where they ever learned in their *salons* and libraries enough of humanity to theorise so boldly, and with such likeness to truth, as they did. It is not merely in the absolute out-of-doors independence of the old-fashioned Gipsy, freer than any wild beast from care for food, that his resemblance to a "philosopher" consists, or rather to the ideal man, free from imaginary cares. For more than this, be it for good or for evil, the real Gipsy has, unlike all other men, unlike the lowest savage, positively no religion, no tie to a spiritual world, no fear of a future, nothing but a few trifling superstitions and legends, which in themselves indicate no faith whatever in anything deeply seated. It would be difficult, I think, for any highly civilised man, who had not studied Thought deeply, and in a liberal spirit, to approach in the least to a rational comprehension of a real Gipsy mind. During my life it has been my fortune to become intimate with men who were "absolutely" or "positively" free-thinkers--men who had, by long study and mere logic, completely freed themselves from any mental tie whatever. Such men are rare; it requires an enormous amount of intellectual culture, an unlimited expenditure of pains in the metaphysical hot-bed, and tremendous self- confidence to produce them--I mean "the real article." Among the most thorough of these, a man on whom utter and entire freedom of thought sat easily and unconsciously, was a certain German doctor of philosophy named P---. To him God and all things were simply ideas of development. The last remark which I can recall from him was "*Ja, ja*. We advanced Hegelians agree exactly on the whole with the Materialists." Now, to my mind, nothing seems more natural than that, when sitting entire days talking with an old Gipsy, no one rises so frequently from the past before me as Mr P---. To him all religion represented a portion of the vast mass of frozen, petrified developments, which simply impede the march of intelligent minds; to my Rommany friend, it is one of the thousand inventions of *gorgio* life, which, like policemen, are simply obstacles to Gipsies in the search of a living, and could he have grasped the circumstances of the case, he would doubtless have replied "*Avali*, we Gipsies agree on the whole exactly with Mr P---." Extremes meet.

One Sunday an old Gipsy was assuring me, with a great appearance of piety, that on that day she neither told fortunes nor worked at any kind of labour--in fact, she kept it altogether correctly.

"*Avali*, *dye*," I replied. "Do you know what the Gipsies in Germany say became of their church?"

"*Kek*," answered the old lady. "No. What is it?"

"They say that the Gipsies' church was made of pork, and the dogs ate it."

Long, loud, and joyously affirmative was the peal of laughter with which the Gipsies welcomed this characteristic story.

So far as research and the analogy of living tribes of the same race can establish a fact, it would seem that the Gipsies were, previous to their quitting India, not people of high caste, but wandering Pariahs, outcasts, foes to the Brahmins, and unbelievers. All the Pariahs are not free-thinkers, but in India, the Church, as in Italy, loses no time in making of all detected free-thinkers Pariahs. Thus we are told, in the introduction to the English translation of that very curious book, "The Tales of the Gooroo Simple," which should be read by every scholar, that all the true literature of the country--that which has life, and freedom, and humour--comes from the Pariahs. And was it different in those days, when Rabelais, and Von Hutten, and Giordano Bruno were, in their wise, Pariahs and Gipsies, roving from city to city, often wanting bread and dreading fire, but asking for nothing but freedom?

The more I have conversed intimately with Gipsies, the more have I been struck by the fact, that my mingled experiences of European education and of life in the Far West of America have given me a basis of mutual intelligence which had otherwise been utterly wanting. I, myself, have known in a wild country what it is to be half-starved for many days--to feel that all my thoughts and intellectual exertions, hour by hour, were all becoming centered on one subject--how to get something to eat. I felt what it was to be wolfish and even ravening; and I noted, step by step, in myself, how a strange sagacity grew within me--an art of detecting food. It was during the American war, and there were thousands of us pitifully starved. When we came near some log hut I began at once to surmise, if I saw a flour sack lying about, that there was a mill not far distant; perhaps flour or bread in the house; while the dwellers in the hut were closely scanned to judge from their appearance if they were well fed, and of a charitable disposition. It is a melancholy thing to recall; but it is absolutely necessary for a thinker to have once lived such a life, that he may be able to understand what is the intellectual status of those fellow beings whose whole life is simply a hunt for enough food to sustain life, and enough beer to cheer it.

I have spoken of the Gipsy fondness for the hedgehog. Richard Liebich, in his book, ***Die Zigeuner in ihrem Wesen und in ihrer Sprache***, tells his readers that the only indication of a belief in a future state which he ever detected in an old Gipsy woman, was that she once dreamed she was in heaven. It appeared to her as a large garden, full of fine fat hedgehogs. "This is," says Mr Liebich, "unquestionably very earthly, and dreamed very sensuously; reminding us of Mahommed's paradise, which in like manner was directed to the animal and not to the spiritual nature, only that here were hedgehogs and there houris."

Six or seven thousand years of hungry-marauding, end by establishing strange points of difference between the mind of a Gipsy and a well-to-do citizen. It has starved God out of the former; he inherited unbelief from his half fed Pariah ancestors, and often retains it, even in England, to this day, with many other unmistakable signs of his Eastern- jackal origin. And strange as it may seem to you, reader, his intercourse with Christians has all over Europe been so limited, that he seldom really knows what religion is. The same Mr Liebich tells us that one day he overheard a Gipsy disputing with his wife as to what was the true character of the belief of the Gentiles. Both admitted that there was a great elder grown up God (the ***baro puro dewel***), and a smaller younger God (the ***tikno tarno dewel***). But the wife maintained, appealing to Mr Liebich for confirmation, that the great God no longer reigned, having abdicated in favour of the Son, while the husband declared that the Great older God died long ago, and that the world was now governed by the little God who was, however, not the son of his predecessor, but of a poor carpenter.

I have never heard of any such nonsense among the English wandering Gipsies with regard to Christianity, but at the same time I must admit that their ideas of what the Bible contains are extremely vague. One day I was sitting with an old Gipsy, discussing Rommany matters, when he suddenly asked me what the word was in the ***waver temmeny jib***, or foreign Gipsy, for The Seven Stars.

"That would be," I said, "the ***Efta Sirnie***. I suppose your name for it is the Hefta Pens. There is a story that once they were seven sisters, but one of them was lost, and so they are called seven to this day--though there are only six. And their right name is the Pleiades."

"That ***gudlo***--that story," replied the gipsy, "is like the one of the Seven Whistlers, which you know is in the Scriptures."

"What!"

"At least they told me so; that the Seven Whistlers are seven spirits of ladies who fly by night, high in the air, like birds. And it says in the Bible that once on a time one got lost, and never came back again, and now the six whistles to find her. But people calls 'em the Seven Whistlers--though there are only six--exactly the same as in your story of the stars."

"It's queer," resumed my Gipsy, after a pause, "how they always tells these here stories by Sevens. Were you ever on Salisbury Plain?"

"No!"

"There are great stones there--***bori bars***--and many a night I've slept there in the moonlight, in the open air, when I was a boy, and listened to my father tellin' me about the Baker. For there's seven great stories, and they say that hundreds of years ago a baker used to come with loaves of bread, and waste it all a tryin' to make seven loaves remain at the same place, one on each stone. But one all'us fell off, and to this here day he's never yet been able to get all seven on the seven stones."

I think that my Gipsy told this story in connection with that of the Whistlers, because he was under the impression that it also was of Scriptural origin. It is, however, really curious that the Gipsy term for an owlet is the ***Maromengro's Chavi***, or Baker's Daughter, and that they are all familiar with the monkish legend which declares that Jesus, in a baker's shop, once asked for bread. The mistress was about to give him a large cake, when her daughter declared it was too much, and diminished the gift by one half.

"He nothing said,
But by the fire laid down the bread,
When lo, as when a blossom blows--
To a vast loaf the manchet rose;
In angry wonder, standing by,
The girl sent forth a wild, rude cry,
And, feathering fast into a fowl,
Flew to the woods a wailing owl."

According to Eilert Sundt, who devoted his life to studying the **Fanten and Tataren**, or vagabonds and Gipsies of Sweden and Norway, there is a horrible and ghastly semblance among them of something like a religion, current in Scandinavia. Once a year, by night, the Gipsies of that country assemble for the purpose of un-baptizing all of their children whom they have, during the year, suffered to be baptized for the sake of gifts, by the Gorgios. On this occasion, amid wild orgies, they worship a small idol, which is preserved until the next meeting with the greatest secrecy and care by their captain. I must declare that this story seems very doubtful to me.

I have devoted this chapter to illustrating from different points the fact that there lives in England a race which has given its impress to a vast proportion of our vagabond population, and which is more curious and more radically distinct in all its characteristics, than our writers, with one or two exceptions, have ever understood. One extraordinary difference still remains to be pointed out--as it has, in fact, already been, with great acumen, by Mr George Borrow, in his "Gipsies in Spain," and by Dr Alexander Paspati, in his "Etudes sur les Tchinghianes ou Bohemiens de l'Empire Ottoman" (Constantinople, 1870); also by Mr Bright, in his "Hungary," and by Mr Simson. It is this, that in every part of the world it is extremely difficult to get Rommany words, even from intelligent gipsies, although they may be willing with all their heart to communicate them. It may seem simple enough to the reader to ask a man "How do you call 'to carry' in your language?" But can the reader understand that a man, who is possibly very much shrewder than himself in reading at a glance many phases of character, and in countless trickeries, should be literally unable to answer such a question? And yet I have met with many such.

The truth is, that there are people in this world who never had such a thing as an abstract idea, let us say even of an apple, plumped suddenly at them--not once in all their lives--and, when it came, the unphilosophical mind could no more grasp it, than the gentleman mentioned by G. H. Lewes (History of Philosophy), could grasp the idea of substance without attribute as presented by Berkeley. The real Gipsy could talk about apples all day, but the sudden demand for the unconnected word, staggers him--at least, until he has had some practice in this, to him, new process. And it is so with other races. Professor Max Muller once told me in conversation, as nearly as I can recollect, that the Mohawk Indian language is extremely rich in declension, every noun having some sixteen or seventeen inflexions of case, but no nominative. One can express one's relations to a father to a most extraordinary extent, among the dilapidated descendants of that once powerful tribe. But such a thing as the abstract idea of *a* father, or of 'father' *pur et simple*, never entered the Mohawk mind, and this is very like the Gipsies.

When a rather wild Gipsy once gives you a word, it must be promptly recorded, for a demand for its repetition at once confuses him. ***On doit saisir le mot echappe au Nomade, et ne pas l'obliger a le repeter, car il le changera selon so, facon***, says Paspati. Unused to abstract efforts of memory, all that he can retain is the sense of his last remark, and very often this is changed with the fleeting second by some associated thought, which materially modifies it. It is always difficult, in consequence, to take down a story in the exact terms which a philologist desires. There are two words for "bad" in English Gipsy, *wafro* and *vessavo*; and I think it must have taken me ten minutes one day to learn, from a by no means dull gipsy, whether the latter word was known to him, or if it were used at all. He got himself into a hopeless tangle in trying to explain the difference between *wafro* and *na-flo*, or ill, until his mind finally refused to act on *vessavo* at all, and spasmodically rejected it. With all the patience of Job, and the meekness of Moses, I awaited my time, and finally obtained my information.

The impatience of such minds in narrative is amusing. Let us suppose that I am asking some ***kushto Rommany chal*** for a version of AEsop's fable of the youth and the cat. He is sitting comfortably by the fire, and good ale has put him into a story-telling humour. I begin--

"Now then, tell me this ***adree Rommanis***, in Gipsy--Once upon a time there was a young man who had a cat."

Gipsy.--" ***Yeckorus--'pre yeck cheirus*** -- *a raklo lelled a matchka*"--

While I am writing this down, and long before it is half done, the professor of Rommany, becoming interested in the subject, continues volubly--

--" ***an' the matchka yeck sala dicked a chillico apre a rukk*** --(and the cat one morning saw a bird in a tree"--)

I.--"Stop, stop! ***Hatch a wongish***! That is not it! Now go on. ***The young man loved this cat so much***"--

Gipsy (fluently, in Rommany), "that he thought her skin would make a nice pair of gloves"--

"Confound your gloves! Now do begin again"--

Gipsy, with an air of grief and injury: "I'm sure I was telling the story for you the best way I knew how!"

Yet this man was far from being a fool. What was it, then? Simply and solely, a lack of education--of that mental training which even those who never entered a schoolhouse, receive more or less of, when they so much as wait patiently for a month behind a chair, or tug for six months at a plough, or in short, acquire the civilised virtue of Christian patience. That is it. We often hear in this world that a little education goes a great way; but to get some idea of the immense value of a very little education indeed, and the incredible effect it may have upon character, one should study with gentleness and patience a real Gipsy.

Probably the most universal error in the world is the belief that all men, due allowance being made for greater or less knowledge, or "talents," have minds like our own; are endowed with the same moral perception, and see things on the whole very much as we do. Now the truth is that a Chinese, whose mind is formed, not by "religion" as we understand it, but simply by the intense pressure of "Old Custom," which we do not understand, thinks in a different manner from an European; moralists accuse him of "moral obliquity," but in reality it is a moral difference. Docility of mind, the patriarchal principle, and the very perfection of innumerable wise and moral precepts have, by the practice of thousands of years, produced in him their natural result. Whenever he attempts to think, his mind runs at once into some broad and open path, beautifully bordered with dry artificial flowers, {21} and the result has been the inability to comprehend any new idea--a state to which the Church of the Middle Ages, or any too rigidly established system, would in a few thousand years have reduced humanity. Under the action of widely different causes, the gipsy has also a different cast of mind from our own, and a radical moral difference. A very few years ago, when I was on the Plains of Western Kansas, old Black Kettle, a famous Indian chief said in a speech, "I am not a white man, I am a ***wolf***. I was born like a wolf on the prairies. I have lived like a wolf, and I shall die like one." Such is the wild gipsy. Ever poor and hungry, theft seems to him, in the trifling easy manner in which he practises it, simply a necessity. The moral aspects of petty crime he never considers at all, nor does he, in fact, reflect upon anything as it is reflected on by the humblest peasant who goes to church, or who in any way feels himself connected as an integral part of that great body-corporate- -Society.

CHAPTER II. A GIPSY COTTAGE.

The Old Fortune-Teller and her Brother.--The Patteran, or Gipsies' Road-Mark .--The Christian Cross, named by Continental Gipsies Trushul, after the Trident of Siva.--Curious English-Gipsy term for the Cross.--Ashwood Fires on Christmas Day.--Our Saviour regarded with affection by the Rommany because he was like themselves and poor.--Strange ideas of the Bible.--The Oak.--Lizards renew their lives.--Snails.--Slugs.--Tobacco Pipes as old as the world.

Duveleste; Avo. Mandy's kaired my patteran adusta chairuses where a drum jals atut the waver," which means in English--"God bless you, yes. Many a time I have marked my sign where the roads cross."

I was seated in the cottage of an old Gipsy mother, one of the most noted fortune-tellers in England, when I heard this from her brother, himself an ancient wanderer, who loves far better to hear the lark sing than the mouse cheep when he wakes of a morning.

It was a very small but clean cottage, of the kind quite peculiar to the English labourer, and therefore attractive to every one who has felt the true spirit of the most original poetry and art which this country has produced. For look high or low, dear reader, you will find that nothing has ever been better done in England than the pictures of rural life, and over nothing have its gifted minds cast a deeper charm.

There were the little rough porcelain figures of which the English peasantry are so fond, and which, cheap as they are, indicate that the taste of your friends Lady --- for Worcester "porcelain," or the Duchess of --- for Majolica, has its roots among far humbler folk. In fact there were perhaps twenty things which no English reader would have supposed were peculiar, yet which were something more than peculiar to me. The master of the house was an Anglo-Saxon--a Gorgio--and his wife, by some magic or other, the oracle before-mentioned.

And I, answering said--

"So you all call it *patteran*?" {24}

"No; very few of us know that name. We do it without calling it anything."

Then I took my stick and marked on the floor the following sign--

"There," I said, "is the oldest patteran--first of all--which the Gipsies use to-day in foreign lands. In Germany, when one band of Gipsies goes by a cross road, they draw that deep in the dust, with the end of the longest line pointing in the direction in which they have gone. Then, the next who come by see the mark, and, if they choose, follow it."

"We make it differently," said the Gipsy. "This is our sign--the *trin bongo drums*, or cross." And he drew his patteran thus--

"The long end points the way," he added; "just as in your sign."

"You call a cross," I remarked, " *trin bongo drums*, or the three crooked roads. Do you know any such word as *trushul* for it?"

"No; *trushilo* is thirsty, and *trushni* means a faggot, and also a basket."

"I shouldn't wonder if a faggot once got the old Rommany word for cross," I said, "because in it every stick is crossed by the wooden *withy* which binds it; and in a basket, every wooden strip crosses the other."

I did not, however, think it worth while to explain to the Gipsies that when their ancestors, centuries ago, left India, it was with the memory that Shiva, the Destroyer, bore a trident, the tri-cula in Sanscrit, the *trisul* of Mahadeva in Hindu-stani, and that in coming to Europe the resemblance of its shape to that of the Cross impressed them, so that they gave to the Christian symbol the name of the sacred triple spear. {26} For if you turn up a little the two arms of a cross, you change the emblem of suffering and innocence at once into one of murder--just as ever so little a deviation from goodness will lead you, my dear boy, into any amount of devilry.

And that the unfailing lucid flash of humour may not be wanting, there lightens on my mind the memory of *The Mysterious Pitchfork*--a German satirical play which made a sensation in its time--and Herlossohn in his romance of *Der Letzte Taborit* (which helped George Sand amazingly in Consuelo), makes a Gipsy chieftain appear in a wonderfully puzzling light by brandishing, in fierce midnight dignity, this agricultural parody on Neptune's weapon, which brings me nicely around to my Gipsies again.

If I said nothing to the inmates of the cottage of all that the *trushul* or cross trident suggested, still less did I vex their souls with the mystic possible meaning of the antique *patteran* or sign which I had drawn. For it has, I opine, a deep meaning, which as one who knew Creuzer of old, I have a right to set forth. Briefly, then, and without encumbering my book with masses of authority, let me state that in all early lore, the *road* is a symbol of life; Christ himself having used it in this sense. Cross roads were peculiarly meaning-full as indicating the meet-of life with life, of good with evil, a faith of which abundant traces are preserved in the fact that until the present generation suicides were buried at them, and magical rites and diabolic incantations are supposed to be most successful when practised in such places. The English *path*, the Gipsy patteran, the Rommany-Hindu *pat*, a foot, and the Hindu *panth*, a road, all meet in the Sanscrit *path*, which was the original parting of the ways. Now the *patteran* which I have drawn, like the Koua of the Chinese or the mystical *Swastika* of the Buddhists, embraces the long line of life, or of the infinite and the short, or broken lines of the finite, and, therefore, as an ancient magical Eastern sign, would be most appropriately inscribed as a *sikker-paskero dromescro*--or hand post--to show the wandering Rommany how to proceed on their way of life.

That the ordinary Christian Cross should be called by the English Gipsies a *trin bongo drum*--or the three cross roads--is not remarkable when we consider that their only association with it is that of a "wayshower," as Germans would call it. To you, reader, it may be that it points the way of eternal life; to the benighted Rommany-English-Hindoo, it indicates nothing more than the same old weary track of daily travel; of wayfare and warfare with the world, seeking food and too often finding none; living for petty joys and driven by dire need; lying down with poverty and rising with hunger, ignorant in his very wretchedness of a thousand things which he *ought* to want, and not knowing enough to miss them.

Just as the reader a thousand, or perhaps only a hundred, years hence--should a copy of this work be then extant--may pity the writer of these lines for his ignorance of the charming comforts, as yet unborn, which will render **his** physical condition so delightful. To thee, oh, future reader, I am what the Gipsy is to me! Wait, my dear boy of the Future--wait--till **you** get to heaven!

Which is a long way off from the Gipsies. Let us return. We had spoken **of patteran**, or of crosses by the way-side, and this led naturally enough to speaking of Him who died on the Cross, and of wandering. And I must confess that it was with great interest I learned that the Gipsies, from a very singular and Rommany point of view, respect, and even pay him, in common with the peasantry in some parts of England, a peculiar honour. For this reason I bade the Gipsy carefully repeat his words, and wrote them down accurately. I give them in the original, with a translation. Let me first state that my informant was not quite clear in his mind as to whether the Boro Divvus, or Great Day, was Christmas or New Year's, nor was he by any means certain on which Christ was born. But he knew very well that when it came, the Gipsies took great pains to burn an ash-wood fire.

"Avali--adusta cheirus I've had to jal dui or trin mees of a Boro Divvus sig' in the sala, to lel ash-wood for the yag. That was when I was a bitti chavo, for my dadas always would keravit.

"An' we kairs it because foki pens our Saviour, the tikno Duvel was born apre the Boro Divvus, 'pre the puv, avree in the temm, like we Rommanis, and he was brought 'pre pash an ash yag--(**Why you can dick dovo adree the Scriptures**!).

"The ivy and holly an' pine rukks never pookered a lav when our Saviour was gaverin' of his kokero, an' so they tools their jivaben saw (sar) the wen, and dicks selno saw the besh; but the ash, like the surrelo rukk, pukkered atut him, where he was gaverin, so they have to hatch mullo adree the wen. And so we Rommany chals always hatchers an ash yag saw the Boro Divvuses. For the tickno duvel was chivved a wadras 'pre the puvius like a Rommany chal, and kistered apre a myla like a Rommany, an' jalled pale the tem a mangin his moro like a Rom. An' he was always a pauveri choro mush, like we, till he was nashered by the Gorgios.

"An' he kistered apre a myla? Avali. Yeckorus he putchered the pash- grai if he might kister her, but she pookered him **kek**. So because the pash-grai wouldn't rikker him, she was sovahalled againsus never to be a dye or lel tiknos. So she never lelled kek, nor any cross either.

"Then he putchered the myla to rikker him, and she penned: 'Avali!' so he pet a cross apre laki's dumo. And to the divvus the myla has a trin bongo drum and latch-ers tiknos, but the pash-grai has kek. So the mylas 'longs of the Rommanis."

(TRANSLATION.)--"Yes--many a time I've had to go two or three miles of a Great Day (Christmas), early in the morning, to get ash-wood for the fire. That was when I was a small boy, for my father always would do it.

"And we do it because people say our Saviour, the small God, was born on the Great Day, in the field, out in the country, like we Rommanis, and he was brought up by an ash-fire."

Here a sudden sensation of doubt or astonishment at my ignorance seemed to occur to my informant, for he said,--

"Why, you can see that in the Scriptures!"

To which I answered, "But the Gipsies have Scripture stories different from those of the Gorgios, and different ideas about religion. Go on with your story. Why do you burn ash-wood?"

"The ivy, and holly, and pine trees, never told a word where our Saviour was hiding himself, and so they keep alive all the winter, and look green all the year. But the ash, like the oak (*lit*. strong tree), told of him (*lit*. across, against him), where he was hiding, so they have to remain dead through the winter. And so we Gipsies always burn an ash- fire every Great Day. For the Saviour was born in the open field like a Gipsy, and rode on an ass like one, and went round the land a begging his bread like a Rom. And he was always a poor wretched man like us, till he was destroyed by the Gentiles.

"And He rode on an ass? Yes. Once he asked the mule if he might ride her, but she told him no. So because the mule would not carry him, she was cursed never to be a mother or have children. So she never had any, nor any cross either.

"Then he asked the ass to carry him, and she said 'Yes;' so he put a cross upon her back. And to this day the ass has a cross and bears young, but the mule has none. So the asses belong to (are peculiar to) the Gipsies."

There was a pause, when I remarked--

"That is a ***fino gudlo***--a fine story; and all of it about an ash tree. Can you tell me anything about the ***surrelo rukk***--the strong tree--the oak?"

"Only what I've often heard our people say about its life."

"And what is that?"

"Dui hundred besh a hatchin, dui hundred besh nasherin his chuckko, dui hundred besh 'pre he mullers, and then he nashers sar his ratt and he's kekoomi kushto." {30}

"That is good, too. There are a great many men who would like to live as long."

"*Tacho*, true. But an old coat can hold out better than a man. If a man gets a hole in him he dies, but his *chukko* (coat) can be *toofered* and *sivved apre* (mended and sewed up) for ever. So, unless a man could get a new life every year, as they say the *hepputs*, the little lizards do, he needn't hope to live like an oak."

"Do the lizards get a new life every year?"

"*Avali*. A *hepput* only lives one year, and then he begins life over again."

"Do snails live as long as lizards?"

"Not when I find 'em rya--if I am hungry. Snails are good eating. {32} You can find plenty on the hedges. When they're going about in the fields or (are found) under wood, they are not good eating. The best are those which are kept, or live through (literally *sleep*) the winter. Take 'em and wash 'em and throw 'em into the kettle, with water and a little salt. The broth's good for the yellow jaundice."

"So you call a snail"--

"A bawris," said the old fortune-teller.

"Bawris! The Hungarian Gipsies call it a *bouro*. But in Germany the Rommanis say stargoli. I wonder why a snail should be a stargoli."

"I know," cried the brother, eagerly. "When you put a snail on the fire it cries out and squeaks just like a little child. Stargoli means 'four cries.'"

I had my doubts as to the accuracy of this startling derivation, but said nothing. The same Gipsy on a subsequent occasion, being asked what he would call a *roan* horse in Rommany, replied promptly--

"A matchno grai"--a fish-horse.

"Why a matchno grai?"

"Because a fish has a roan (*i.e.*, roe), hasn't it? Leastways I can't come no nearer to it, if it ain't that."

But he did better when I was puzzling my brain, as the learned Pott and Zippel had done before me, over the possible origin of churro or tchurro, "a ball, or anything round," when he suggested--

"Rya--I should say that as a ***churro*** is round, and a ***curro*** or cup is round, and they both sound alike and look alike, it must be all werry much the same thing." {33}

"Can you tell me anything more about snails?" I asked, reverting to a topic which, by the way, I have observed is like that of the hedgehog, a favourite one with Gipsies.

"Yes; you can cure warts with the big black kind that have no shells."

"You mean slugs. I never knew they were fit to cure anything."

"Why, that's one of the things that everybody knows. When you get a wart on your hands, you go on to the road or into the field till you find a slug, one of the large kind with no shell (literally, with no house upon him), and stick it on the thorn of a blackthorn in a hedge, and as the snail dies, one day after the other, for four or five days, the wart will die away. Many a time I've told that to Gorgios, and Gorgios have done it, and the warts have gone away (literally, cleaned away) from their hands." {34}

Here the Gipsy began to inquire very politely if smoking were offensive to me; and as I assured him that it was not, he took out his pipe. And knowing by experience that nothing is more conducive to sociability, be it among Chippeways or Gipsies, than that smoking which is among our Indians, literally a burnt-offering, {35} I produced a small clay pipe of the time of Charles the Second, given to me by a gentleman who has the amiable taste to collect such curiosities, and give them to his friends under the express condition that they shall be smoked, and not laid away as relics of the past. If you move in ***etching*** circles, dear readers, you will at once know to whom I refer.

The quick eye of the Gipsy at once observed my pipe.

"That is a ***crow-swagler***--a crow-pipe," he remarked.

"Why a crow-pipe?"

"I don't know. Some Gipsies call 'em ***mullos' swaglers***, or dead men's pipes, because those who made 'em were dead long ago. There are places in England where you can find 'em by dozens in the fields. I never dicked (saw) one with so long a stem to it as yours. And they're old, very old. What is it you call it before everything" (here he seemed puzzled for a word) "when the world was a-making?"

"The Creation."

"Avali--that's it, the Creation. Well, them crow-swaglers was kaired at the same time; they're hundreds--avali--thousands of beshes (years) old. And sometimes we call the beng (devil) a swagler, or we calls a swagler the beng."

"Why?"

"Because the devil lives in smoke."

CHAPTER III. THE GIPSY TINKER.

Difficulty of coming to an Understanding with Gipsies.--The Cabman.--
Rommany for French.--"Wanderlust."--Gipsy Politeness.--The Tinker and
the Painting.--Secrets of Bat-catching.--The Piper of Hamelin, and the Tinker's Opinion of the Story.--The Walloon Tinker of Spa.--Argot.

O ne summer day in London, in 1871, I was seated alone in an artist's
studio. Suddenly I heard without, beneath the window, the murmur of
two voices, and the sleepy, hissing, grating sound of a scissors-grinder's
wheel.

By me lay a few tools, one of which, a chisel, was broken. I took it, went softly
to the window, and looked down.

There was the wheel, including all the apparatus of a travelling tinker. I looked
to see if I could discover in the two men who stood by it any trace of the Rommany. One, a fat, short, mind-his-own-business, ragged son of the roads, who looked,
however, as if a sturdy drinker might be hidden in his shell, was evidently not my
"affair." He seemed to be the "Co." of the firm.

But by him, and officiating at the wheeling smithy, stood a taller figure--the
face to me invisible--which I scrutinised more nearly. And the instant I observed
his *hat* I said to myself, "This looks like it."

For dilapidated, worn, wretched as that hat was, there was in it an attempt,
though indescribably humble, to be something melo-dramatic, foreign, Bohemian,
and poetic. It was the mere blind, dull, dead germ of an effort--not even *life*--only
the ciliary movement of an antecedent embryo--and yet it *had* got beyond Anglo-
Saxondom. No costermonger, or common cad, or true Englishman, ever yet had
that indefinable touch of the opera-supernumerary in the streets. It *was* a som-

brero.

"That's the man for me," I said. So I called him, and gave him the chisel, and after a while went down. He was grinding away, and touched his hat respectfully as I approached.

Now the reader is possibly aware that of all difficult tasks one of the most difficult is to induce a disguised Gipsy, or even a professed one, to utter a word of Rommany to a man not of the blood. Of this all writers on the subject have much to say. For it is so black-swanish, I may say so centenarian in unfrequency, for a gentleman to speak Gipsy, that the Zingaro thus addressed is at once subjected to morbid astonishment and nervous fears, which under his calm countenance and infinite "cheek" are indeed concealed, but which speedily reduce themselves to two categories.

1. That Rommany is the language of men at war with the law; therefore you are either a detective who has acquired it for no healthy purpose, or else yourself are a scamp so high up in the profession that it behooves all the little fish of outlawdom to beware of you.

2. Or else--what is quite as much to be dreaded--you are indeed a gentleman, but one seeking to make fun of him, and possibly able to do so. At any rate, your knowledge of Rommany is a most alarming coin of vantage. Certainly, reader, you know that a regular London streeter, say a cabman, would rather go to jail than be beaten in a chaffing match. I nearly drove a hansom into sheer convulsions one night, about the time this chapter happened, by a very light puzzler indeed. I had hesitated between him and another.

"You don't know ***your own mind***," said the disappointed candidate to me.

"***Mind your own*** business," I replied. It was a poor palindrome, {38} reader--hardly worth telling--yet it settled him. But he swore--oh, of course he did--he swore beautifully.

Therefore, being moved to caution, I approached calmly and gazed earnestly on the revolving wheel.

"Do you know," I said, "I think a great deal of your business, and take a great interest in it."

"Yes, sir."

"I can tell you all the names of your tools in French. You'd like to hear them, wouldn't you?"

"Wery much indeed, sir."

So I took up the chisel. "This," I said, "is a ***churi***, sometimes called a ***chino-mescro***."

"That's the French for it, is it, sir?" replied the tinker, gravely. Not a muscle of his face moved.

"The ***coals***," I added, "are ***hangars*** or ***wongurs***, sometimes called ***kaulos***."

"Never heerd the words before in my life," quoth the sedate tinker.

"The bellows is a ***pudemengro***. Some call it a ***pishota***."

"Wery fine language, sir, is French," rejoined the tinker. In every instance he repeated the words after me, and pronounced them correctly, which I had not invariably done. "Wery fine language. But it's quite new to me."

"You wouldn't think now," I said, affably, "that *I* had ever been on the roads!"

The tinker looked at me from my hat to my boots, and solemnly replied--

"I should say it was wery likely. From your language, sir, wery likely indeed."

I gazed as gravely back as if I had not been at that instant the worst sold man in London, and asked--

"Can you ***rakher Rommanis***?" (***i.e.***, speak Gipsy.)

And *he* said he *could*.

Then we conversed. He spoke English intermingled with Gipsy, stopping from time to time to explain to his assistant, or to teach him a word. This portly person appeared to be about as well up in the English Gipsy as myself--that is, he knew it quite as imperfectly. I learned that the master had been in America, and made New York and Brooklyn glad by his presence, while Philadelphia, my native city had been benefited as to its scissors and morals by him.

"And as I suppose you made money there, why didn't you remain?" I inquired.

The Gipsy--for he was really a Gipsy, and not a half-scrag--looked at me wistfully, and apparently a little surprised that I should ask him such a question.

"Why, sir, *you* know that *we* can't keep still. Somethin' kept telling me to move on, and keep a movin'. Some day I'll go back again."

Suddenly--I suppose because a doubt of my perfect Freemasonry had been aroused by my absurd question--he said, holding up a kettle--

"What do you call this here in Rommanis?"

"I call it a **kekavi** or a **kavi**," I said. "But it isn't **right** Rommany. It's Greek, which the Rommanichals picked up on their way here."

And here I would remark, by the way, that I have seldom spoken to a Gipsy in England who did not try me on the word for kettle.

"And what do you call a face?" he added.

"I call a face a **mui**," I said, "and a nose a **nak**; and as for **mui**, I call **rikker tiro mui**, 'hold your jaw.' That is German Rommany."

The tinker gazed at me admiringly, and then said, "You're 'deep' Gipsy, I see, sir--that's what **you** are."

"*Mo rov a jaw*; *mo rakker so drovan*?" I answered. "Don't talk so loud; do you think I want all the Gorgios around here to know I talk Gipsy? Come in; *jal adree the ker and pi a curro levinor*."

The tinker entered. As with most Gipsies there was really, despite the want of "education," a real politeness--a singular intuitive refinement pervading all his actions, which indicated, through many centuries of brutalisation, that fountain-source of all politeness--the Oriental. Many a time I have found among Gipsies whose life, and food, and dress, and abject ignorance, and dreadful poverty were far below that of most paupers and prisoners, a delicacy in speaking to and acting before ladies, and a tact in little things, utterly foreign to the great majority of poor Anglo-Saxons, and not by any means too common in even higher classes.

For example, there was a basket of cakes on the table, which cakes were made like soldiers in platoons. Now Mr Katzimengro, or Scissorman, as I call him, not being familiar with the anatomy of such delicate and winsome maro, or bread, was startled to find, when he picked up one biscuit de Rheims, that he had taken a row. Instantly he darted at me an astonished and piteous glance, which said--

"I cannot, with my black tinker fingers, break off and put the cakes back again; I do not want to take all--it looks greedy."

So I said, "Put them in your pocket." And he did so, quietly. I have never seen anything done with a better grace.

On the easel hung an unfinished picture, representing the Piper of Hamelin surrounded by rats without number. The Gipsy appeared to be much interested in it.

"I used to be a rat-catcher myself," he said. "I learned the business under old Lee, who was the greatest rat-catcher in England. I suppose you know, of course, sir, how to *draw* rats?"

"Certainly," I replied. "Oil of rhodium. I have known a house to be entirely cleared by it. There were just thirty-six rats in the house, and they had a trap which held exactly twelve. For three nights they caught a dozen, and that finished the congregation."

"Aniseed is better," replied the Gipsy, solemnly. (By the way, another and an older Gipsy afterwards told me that he used caraway-oil and the heads of dried herrings.) "And if you've got a rat, sir, anywhere in this here house, I'll bring it to you in five minutes."

He did, in fact, subsequently bring the artist as models for the picture two very pretty rats, which he had quite tamed while catching them.

"But what does the picture mean, sir?" he inquired, with curiosity.

"Once upon a time," I replied, "there was a city in Germany which was over-run with rats. They teased the dogs and worried the cats, and bit the babies in the cradle, and licked the soup from the cook's own ladle."

"There must have been an uncommon lot of them, sir," replied the tinker, gravely.

"There was. Millions of them. Now in those days there were no Rommanichals, and consequently no rat-catchers."

"'Taint so now-a-days," replied the Gipsy, gloomily. "The business is quite spiled, and not to get a livin' by."

"Avo. And by the time the people had almost gone crazy, one day there came a man--a Gipsy--the first Gipsy who had ever been seen in *dovo tem* (or that country). And he agreed for a thousand crowns to clear all the rats away. So he blew on a pipe, and the rats all followed him out of town."

"What did he blow on a pipe for?"

"Just for *hokkerben*, to humbug them. I suppose he had oils rubbed on his heels. But when he had drawn the rats away and asked for his money, they would not give it to him. So then, what do you think he did?"

"I suppose--ah, I see," said the Gipsy, with a shrewd look. "He went and drew 'em all back again."

"No; he went, and this time piped all the children away. They all went after him--all except one little lame boy--and that was the last of it."

The Gipsy looked earnestly at me, and then, as if I puzzled, but with an expression of perfect faith, he asked--

"And is that all *tacho*--all a fact--or is it made up, you know?"

"Well, I think it is partly one and partly the other. You see, that in those days Gipsies were very scarce, and people were very much astonished at rat-drawing, and so they made a queer story of it."

"But how about the children?"

"Well," I answered; "I suppose you have heard occasionally that Gipsies used to chore Gorgios' chavis--steal people's children?"

Very grave indeed was the assent yielded to this explanation. He *had* heard it among other things.

My dear Mr Robert Browning, I little thought, when I suggested to the artist your poem of the piper, that I should ever retail the story in Rommany to a tinker. But who knows with whom he may associate in this life, or whither he may drift on the great white rolling sea of humanity? Did not Lord Lytton, unless the preface to Pelham err, himself once tarry in the tents of the Egyptians? and did not Christopher North also wander with them, and sing--

"Oh, little did my mother think,   The day she cradled me,   The lands that I should travel in,   Or the death that I should dee;   Or gae rovin' about wi' tinkler loons,   And sic-like companie"?

"You know, sir," said the Gipsy, "that we have two languages. For besides the Rummany, there's the reg'lar cant, which all tinkers talk."

"*Kennick* you mean?"

"Yes, sir; that's the Rummany for it. A 'dolly mort' is Kennick, but it's *juva* or *rakli* in Rummanis. It's a girl, or a rom's *chi*."

"You say *rom* sometimes, and then *rum*."

"There's *rums* and *roms*, sir. The *rum* is a Gipsy, and a *rom* is a husband."

"That's your English way of calling it. All the rest of the world over there is only one word among Gipsies, and that is *rom*."

Now, the allusion to *Kennick* or cant by a tinker, recalls an incident which, though not strictly Gipsy in its nature, I will nevertheless narrate.

In the summer of 1870 I spent several weeks at Spa, in the Ardennes. One day while walking I saw by the roadside a picturesque old tinker, looking neither better nor worse than the grinder made immortal by Teniers.

I was anxious to know if all of his craft in Belgium could speak Gipsy, and addressed him in that language, giving him at the same time my knife to grind. He replied politely in French that he did not speak Rommany, and only understood French and Walloon. Yet he seemed to understand perfectly the drift of my question, and to know what Gipsy was, and its nature, since after a pause he added, with a significant smile--

"But to tell the truth, monsieur, though I cannot talk Rommany, I know another secret language. I can speak *Argot* fluently."

Now, I retain in my memory, from reading the Memoirs of Vidocq thirty years ago, one or two phrases of this French thieves' slang, and I at once replied that I knew a few words of it myself, adding--

"*Tu sais jaspiner en bigorne*?"--you can talk argot?

"*Oui, monsieur*."

"*Et tu vas roulant de vergne en vergne*?"--and you go about from town to town?

Grave and keen, and with a queer smile, the tinker replied, very slowly--

"Monsieur knows the Gipsies" (here he shook his head), "and monsieur speaks *argot* very well." (A shrug.) "Perhaps he knows more than he credits himself with. Perhaps" (and here his wink was diabolical)-- "*perhaps monsieur knows the entire tongue*!"

Spa is full not only of gamblers, but of numbers of well-dressed Parisian sharpers who certainly know "the entire tongue." I hastened to pay my tinker, and went my way homewards. Ross Browne was accused in Syria of having "burgled" onions, and the pursuit of philology has twice subjected me to be suspected by tinkers as a flourishing member of the "dangerous classes."

But to return to my rat-catcher. As I quoted a verse of German Gipsy song, he manifested an interest in it, and put me several questions with regard to the race in other lands.

"I wish I was a rich gentleman. I would like to travel like you, sir, and have nothing to do but go about from land to land, looking after our Rummany people as you do, and learnin' everything Rummany. Is it true, sir, we come from Egypt?"

"No. I think not. There are Gipsies in Egypt, but there is less Rommany in their *jib* (language) than in any other Gipsy tribe in the world. The Gipsies came from India."

"And don't you think, sir, that we're of the children of the lost Ten Tribes?"

"I am quite sure that you never had a drop of blood in common with them. Tell me, do you know any Gipsy *gilis*--any songs?"

"Only a bit of a one, sir; most of it isn't fit to sing, but it begins--"

And here he sang:

"Jal 'dree the ker my honey,   And you shall be my rom."

And chanting this, after thanking me, he departed, gratified with his gratuity, rejoiced at his reception, and most undoubtedly benefited by the beer with which I had encouraged his palaver--a word, by the way, which is not inappropriate, since it contains in itself the very word of words, the *lav*, which means a word, and is most antiquely and excellently Gipsy. Pehlevi is old Persian, and to *pen lavi* is Rommany all the world over "to speak words."

CHAPTER IV. GIPSY RESPECT FOR THE DEAD.

Gipsies and Comteists identical as to "Religion"--Singular Manner of Mourning for the Dead, as practised by Gipsies--Illustrations from Life--Gipsy Job and the Cigars--Oaths by the Dead--Universal Gipsy Custom of never Mentioning the Names of the Dead--Burying valuable Objects with the Dead--Gipsies, Comteists, Hegelians, and Jews--The Rev. James Crabbe.

Comte, the author of the Positivist philosophy, never felt the need of a religion until he had fallen in love; and at the present day his "faith" appears to consist in a worship of the great and wise and good among the dead. I have already spoken of many Gipsies reminding me, by their entirely unconscious ungodliness, of thorough Hegelians. I may now add, that, like the Positivists, they seem to correct their irreligion through the influence of love; and by a strange custom, which is, in spirit and fact, nothing less than adoring the departed and offering to the dead a singular sacrifice.

He who has no house finds a home in family and friends, whence it results that the Gipsy, despite his ferocious quarrels in the clan, and his sharp practice even with near relations, is--all things considered--perhaps the most devoted to kith and kin of any one in the world. His very name--rom, a husband--indicates it. His children, as almost every writer on him, from Grellmann down to the present day, has observed, are more thoroughly indulged and spoiled than any non-gipsy can conceive; and despite all the apparent contradictions caused by the selfishness born of poverty, irritable Eastern blood, and the eccentricity of semi-civilisation, I doubt if any man, on the whole, in the world, is more attached to his own.

It was only three or four hours ago, as I write, on the fifth day of February 1872, that a Gipsy said to me, "It is nine years since my wife died, and I would give all

Anglaterra to have her again."

That the real religion of the Gipsies, as I have already observed, consists like that of the Comteists, in devotion to the dead, is indicated by a very extraordinary custom, which, notwithstanding the very general decay, of late years, of all their old habits, still prevails universally. This is the refraining from some usage or indulgence in honour of the departed--a sacrifice, as it were, to their *manes*--and I believe that, by inquiring, it will be found to exist among all Gipsies in all parts of the world. In England it is shown by observances which are maintained at great personal inconvenience, sometime for years, or during life. Thus, there are many Gipsies who, because a deceased brother was fond of spirits, have refrained, after his departure, from tasting them, or who have given up their favourite pursuits, for the reason that they were last indulged in, in company with the lost and loved one.

As a further illustration, I will give in the original Gipsy-language, as I myself took it down rapidly, but literally, the comments of a full-blooded Gipsy on this custom--the translation being annexed. I should state that the narrative which precedes his comments was a reply to my question, Why he invariably declined my offer of cigars?

"No; I never toovs cigaras, kek. I never toovs 'em kenna since my pal's chavo Job mullered. And I'll pooker tute how it welled."

"It was at the boro wellgooro where the graias prasters. I was kairin the paiass of the koshters, and mandy dicked a rye an' pookered him for a droppi levinor. '*Avali*,' he penned, 'I'll del you levinor and a kushto tuvalo too.' 'Parraco,' says I, 'rya.' So he del mandy the levinor and a dozen cigaras. I pet em adree my poachy an' jailed apre the purge and latched odoi my pal's chavo, an' he pook'd mandy, 'Where you jallin to, kako?' And I penned: 'Job, I've lelled some covvas for tute.' 'Tacho,' says he--so I del him the cigaras. Penned he: 'Where did tute latcher 'em?' 'A rye del 'em a mandy.' So he pet em adree his poachy, an' pookered mandy, 'What'll tu lel to pi?' 'A droppi levinor.' So he penned, 'Pauli the grais prasters, I'll jal atut the puvius and dick tute.'

"Eight or nine divvuses pauli, at the K'allis's Gav, his pal welled to mandy and pookered mi Job sus naflo. And I penned, 'Any thing dush?' 'Worse nor dovo.' 'What *is* the covvo?' Says yuv, 'Mandy kaums tute to jal to my pal--don't spare the gry--mukk her jal!' So he del mi a fino grai, and I kistered eight mee so sig that

I thought I'd mored her. An' I pet her dree the stanya, an' I jalled a lay in the puv and' odoi I dicked Job. 'Thank me Duvel!' penned he, 'Kako you's welled acai, and if mandy gets opre this bugni (for 'twas the bugni he'd lelled), I'll del tute the kushti-est gry that you'll beat sar the Romni chuls.' But he mullered.

"And he pens as he was mullerin. 'Kako, tute jins the cigarras you del a mandy?' '*Avali*,' I says he, 'I've got 'em acai in my poachy.' Mandy and my pens was by him, but his romni was avree, adree the boro tan, bikinin covvas, for she'd never lelled the bugni, nor his chavos, so they couldn't well a dickin, for we wouldn't mukk em. And so he mullered.

"And when yuv's mullo I pet my wast adree his poachy and there mandy last-ered the cigaras. And from dovo chairus, rya, mandy never tooved a cigar.

"Avali--there's adusta Romni chuls that kairs dovo. And when my juvo mullered, mandy never lelled nokengro kekoomi. Some chairuses in her jivaben, she'd lel a bitti nokengro avree my mokto, and when I'd pen, 'Deari juvo, what do you kair dovo for?' she pooker mandy, 'It's kushti for my sherro.' And so when she mullered mandy never lelled chichi sensus.

"Some mushis wont haw mass because the pal or pen that mullered was kam-maben to it,--some wont pi levinor for panj or ten besh, some wont haw the kam-maben matcho that the chavo hawed. Some wont haw puvengroes or pi tood, or haw pabos, and saw (sar) for the mullos.

"Some won't kair wardos or kil the boshomengro--'that's mandy's pooro chavo's gilli'--and some won't kel. 'No, I can't kel, the last time I kelled was with mandy's poor juvo that's been mullo this shtor besh.'

"'Come pal, let's jal an' have a drappi levinor--the boshomengri's odoi.' 'Kek, pal, kekoomi--I never pi'd a drappi levinor since my bibi's jalled.' 'Kushto--lel some tuvalo pal?' 'Kek--kek--mandy never tooved since minno juvo pelled a lay in the panni, and never jalled avree kekoomi a jivaben.' 'Well, let's jal and kair paiass with the koshters--we dui'll play you dui for a pint o' levinor.' 'Kek--I never kaired the paiass of the koshters since my dadas mullered--the last chairus I ever played was with him.'

"And Lena, the juva of my pal's chavo, Job, never hawed plums a'ter her rom mullered."

(TRANSLATION).--"No, I never smoke cigars. No; I never smoke them now since my brother's son Job died. And I'll tell you how it came.

"It was at the great fair where the horses run (*i.e*., the races), I was keeping a cock-shy, and I saw a gentleman, and asked him for a drop of ale. 'Yes,' he said, 'I'll give you ale, and a good smoke too.' 'Thank you,' says I, 'Sir.' So he gave me the ale, and a dozen cigars. I put them in my pocket, and went on the road and found there my brother's son, and he asked me, 'Where (are) you going, uncle?' And I said: 'Job, I have something for you.' 'Good,' says he--so I gave him the cigars. He said: 'Where did you find them?' 'A gentleman gave them to me.' So he put them in his pocket, and asked me, 'What'll you take to drink?' 'A drop of ale.' So he said, 'After the horses (have) run I'll go across the field and see you.'

"Eight or nine days after, at Hampton Court, {53} his 'pal' came to me and told me that Job was ill. And I said, 'Anything wrong?' 'Worse nor that.' 'What *is* the affair?' Said he, 'I want you to go to my pal,--don't spare the horse--let her go!' So he gave me a fine horse, and I rode eight miles so fast that I thought I'd killed her. And I put her in the stable, and I went down into the field, and there I saw Job. 'Thank God!' said he; 'Uncle, you've come here; and if I get over this small-pox (for 'twas the smallpox he'd caught), I'll give you the best horse that you'll beat all the Gipsies.' But he died.

"And he says as he was dying, 'Uncle, you know the cigars you gave me?' 'Yes.' Says he, 'I've got 'em here in my pocket.' I and my sisters were by him, but his wife was outside in the great tent, selling things, for she never had the smallpox, nor his children, so they couldn't come to see, for we wouldn't let them. And so he died.

"And when he was dead, I put my hand in his pocket, and there I found the cigars. And from that time, Sir, I never smoked a cigar.

"Yes! there are plenty of Gipsies who do that. And when my wife died, I never took snuff again. Sometimes in her life she'd take a bit of snuff out (from) my box; and when I'd say, 'Dear wife, what do you do that for?' she'd tell me, 'It's good for my head.' And so when she died I never took any (none) since.

"Some men won't eat meat because the brother or sister that died was fond of (to) it; some won't drink ale for five or ten years; some won't eat the favourite fish that the child ate. Some won't eat potatoes, or drink milk, or eat apples; and all for the dead.

"Some won't play cards or the fiddle--'that's my poor boy's tune'--and some won't dance--'No, I can't dance, the last time I danced was with my poor wife (or girl) that's been dead this four years.'

"'Come, brother, let's go and have a drop of ale; the fiddler is there.' 'No, brother, I never drank a drop of ale since my aunt went (died).' 'Well, take some tobacco, brother?' 'No, no, I have not smoked since my wife fell in the water and never came out again alive.' 'Well, let's go and play at cock-shy, we two'll play you two for a pint o' ale.' 'No, I never played at cock-shy since my father died; the last time I played was with him.'

"And Lena, the wife of my nephew Job, never ate plums after her husband died."

This is a strange manner of mourning, but it is more effective than the mere wearing of black, since it is often a long-sustained and trying tribute to the dead. Its Oriental-Indian origin is apparent enough. But among the German Gipsies, who, I am firmly convinced, represent in language and customs their English brethren as the latter were three centuries ago, this reverence for the departed assumes an even deeper and more serious character. Mr Richard Liebich (***Die Zigeuner***, ***Leipzig***, 1863), tells us that in his country their most sacred oath is ***Ap i mulende***!--by the dead!--and with it may be classed the equally patriarchal imprecation, "By my father's hand!"

Since writing the foregoing sentence a very remarkable confirmation of the existence of this oath among English Gipsies, and the sacredness with which it is observed, came under my own observation. An elderly Gipsy, during the course of a family difficulty, declared to his sister that he would leave the house. She did not believe he would until he swore by his dead wife--by his "***mullo juvo***." And when he had said this, his sister promptly remarked: "Now you have sworn by her, I know you will do it." He narrated this to me the next day, adding that he was going to put a tent up, about a mile away, and live there. I asked him if he ever swore by his dead father, to which he said: "Always, until my wife died." This poor man was almost entirely ignorant of what was in the Bible, as I found by questioning him; but I doubt whether I know any Christian on whom a Bible oath would be more binding than was to him his own by the dead. To me there was something deeply moving in the simple earnestness and strangeness of this adjuration.

The German, like the older English Gipsies, carefully burn the clothes and bed of the deceased, and, indeed, most objects closely connected with them, and what is more extraordinary, evince their respect by carefully avoiding mentioning their names, even when they are borne by other persons or are characteristic of certain things. So that when a Gipsy maiden named Forella once died, her entire nation, among whom the trout had always been known only by its German designation, Forelle, at once changed the name, and, to this day it is called by them ***mulo madscho*** --the dead fish,--or at times ***lolo madscho*** --the red fish.

This is also the case among the English Gipsies. Wishing to have the exact words and views of a real Rommany on this subject, I made inquiry, and noted down his reply, which was literally as follows:--

"Avali; when Rommany chals or juvos are mullos, their pals don't kaum to shoon their navs pauli--it kairs 'em too bongo--so they're purabend to waver navs. Saw don't kair it--kek--but posh do, kenna. My chavo's nav was Horfer or Horferus, but the bitti chavis penned him Wacker. Well, yeck divvus pre the wellgooro o' the graias prasters, my juvo dicked a boro ***doll*** adree some hev of a buttika and penned, 'Dovo odoi dicks just like moro Wacker!' So we penned him ***Wackerdoll***, but a'ter my juvo mullered I rakkered him Wacker again, because Wackerdoll pet mandy in cammoben o' my poor juvo."

In English: "Yes. When Gipsy men or women die, their friends don't care to hear their names again--it makes them too sad, so they are changed to other names. All don't do it--no--but half of them do so still. My boy's name was Horfer or Horferus (Orpheus), but the children called him Wacker. Well, one day at the great fair of the races, my wife saw a large doll in some window of a shop, and said, 'That looks just like our Wacker!' So we called him Wackerdoll, but after my wife died I called him Wacker again, because Wacker ***doll*** put me in mind of my poor wife."

When further interrogated on the same subject, he said:

"A'ter my juva mullered, if I dicked a waver rakli with lakis'nav, an' mandy was a rakkerin laki, mandy'd pen ajaw a waver geeri's nav, an rakker her by a waver nav:--dovo's to pen I'd lel some bongonav sar's Polly or Sukey. An' it was the sar covva with my dades nav--if I dicked a mush with a nav that simmed leskers, mandy'd rakker him by a waver nav. For 'twould kair any mush wafro to shoon the navyas of the mullas a't 'were cammoben to him."

Or in English, "After my wife died, if I saw another girl with her name, and I was talking to her, I'd *speak* another woman's name, and call her by another name; that's to say, I'd take some nick-name, such as Polly or Sukey. And it was the same thing with my father's name--if I saw a man with a name that was the same as his (literally, 'that *samed* his'), I'd call him by another name. For 'twould make any man grieve (lit. 'bad') to hear the names of the dead that were dear to him."

I suppose that there are very few persons, not of Gipsy blood, in England, to whom the information will not be new, that there are to be found everywhere among us, people who mourn for their lost friends in this strange and touching manner.

Another form of respect for the departed among Gipsies, is shown by their frequently burying some object of value with the corpse, as is, however, done by most wild races. On questioning the same Gipsy last alluded to, he spoke as follows on this subject, I taking down his words:--

"When Job mullered and was chivved adree the puv, there was a nevvi kushtodickin dui chakkas pakkered adree the mullo mokto. Dighton penned a mandy the waver divvus, that trin thousand bars was gavvered posh yeck o' the Chilcotts. An I've shooned o' some Stanleys were buried with sonnakai wongashees apre langis wastos. '*Do sar the Rommany chals kair adovo*?' Kek. Some chivs covvas pash the mullos adree the puv, and boot adusta don't."

In English: "When Job died and was buried, there was a new beautiful pair of shoes put in the coffin (*lit*. corpse-box). Dighton told me the other day, that three thousand pounds were hidden with one of the Chilcotts. And I have heard of some Stanleys who were buried with gold rings on their fingers. '*Do all the Gipsies do that*?' No! some put things with the dead in the earth, and many do not."

Mr Liebich further declares, that while there is really nothing in it to sustain the belief, this extraordinary reverence and regard for the dead is the only fact at all indicating an idea of the immortality of the soul which he has ever found among the Gipsies; but, as he admits, it proves nothing. To me, however, it is grimly grotesque, when I return to the disciples of Comte--the Positivists--the most highly cultivated scholars of the most refined form of philosophy in its latest stage, and find that their ultimate and practical manifestation of *la religion*, is quite the same as that of those unaffected and natural Positivists, the Gipsies. With these, as with the others, our fathers find their immortality in our short-lived memories, and if among either, some one moved by deep love--as Auguste was by the eyes of Clotilda--has yearned for immortality with the dear one, and cursed in agony Annihilation, he falls upon the faith founded in ancient India, that only that soul lives for ever which has done so much good on earth, as to leave behind it in humanity, ineffaceable traces of its elevation.

Verily, the poor Gipsies would seem, to a humourist, to have been created by the devil, whose name they almost use for God, a living parody and satanic burlesque of all that human faith, doubt, or wisdom, have ever accomplished in their highest forms. Even to the weakest minded and most uninformed manufacturers of "Grellmann-diluted" pamphlets, on the Gipsies, their parallel to the Jews is most apparent. All over the world this black and God-wanting shadow dances behind the solid Theism of "The People," affording proof that if the latter can be preserved, even in the wildest wanderings, to illustrate Holy Writ--so can gipsydom--for no apparent purpose whatever. How often have we heard that the preservation of the Jews is a phenomenon without equal? And yet they both live--the sad and sober Jew, the gay and tipsy Gipsy, Shemite and Aryan--the one so ridiculously like and unlike the other, that we may almost wonder whether Humour does not enter into the Divine purpose and have its place in the Destiny of Man. For my own part, I shall always believe that the Heathen Mythology shows a superiority to any other, in *one* conception--that of Loki, who into the tremendous upturnings of the Universe always inspires a grim grotesqueness; a laughter either diabolic or divine.

Judaism, which is pre-eminently the principle of religious belief:--the metaphysical emancipation and enlightenment of Germany, and the materialistic positivism of France, are then, as I have indicated, nowhere so practically and yet laughably illustrated as by the Gipsy. Free from all the trammels of faith, and, to the last degree, indifferent and rationalistic, he satisfies the demands of Feuerbach; devoted to the positive and to the memory of the dead, he is the ideal of the greatest French philosophy, while as a wanderer on the face of the earth--not neglectful of picking up things *en route*--he is the rather blurred *facsimile* of the Hebrew, the main difference in the latter parallel being that while the Jews are God's chosen people, the poor Gipsies seem to have been selected as favourites by that darker spirit, whose name they have naively substituted for divinity:-- *Nomen et omen*.

I may add, however, in due fairness, that there are in England some true Gipsies of unmixed blood, who--it may be without much reflection--have certainly adopted ideas consonant with a genial faith in immortality, and certain phases of religion. The reader will find in another chapter a curious and beautiful Gipsy custom recorded, that of burning an ash fire on Christmas-day, in honour of our Saviour, because He was born and lived like a Gipsy; and one day I was startled by bearing a Rom say "Miduvel hatch for mandy an' kair me kushto."--My God stand up for me and make me well. "That" he added, in an explanatory tone, "is what you say when you're sick." These instances, however, indicate no deep-seated conviction, though they are certainly curious, and, in their extreme simplicity, affecting. That truly good man, the Rev. James Crabb, in his touching little book, "The Gipsies' Advocate," gave numbers of instances of Gipsy conversions to religion and of real piety among them, which occurred after their minds and feelings had been changed by his labours; indeed, it would seem as if their lively imaginations and warm hearts render them extremely susceptible to the sufferings of Jesus. But this does not in the least affect the extraordinary truth that in their nomadic and natural condition, the Gipsies, all the world over, present the spectacle, almost without a parallel, of total indifference to, and ignorance of, religion, and that I have found true old-fashioned specimens of it in England.

I would say, in conclusion, that the Rev. James Crabb, whose unaffected and earnest little book tells its own story, did much good in his own time and way among the poor Gipsies; and the fact that he is mentioned to the present day, by them, with respect and love, proves that missionaries are not useless, nor Gipsies ungrateful--though it is almost the fashion with too many people to assume both positions as rules without exceptions.

CHAPTER V. GIPSY LETTERS.

A Gipsy's Letter to his Sister.--Drabbing Horses.--Fortune Telling.--Cock Shys.--"Hatch 'em pauli, or he'll lel sar the Covvas!"--Two German Gipsy Letters.

I shall give in this chapter a few curious illustrations of Gipsy life and character, as shown in a letter, which is illustrated by two specimens in the German Rommany dialect.

With regard to the first letter, I might prefix to it, as a motto, old John Willett's remark: "What's a man without an imagination?" Certainly it would not apply to the Gipsy, who has an imagination so lively as to be at times almost ungovernable; considering which I was much surprised that, so far as I know, the whole race has as yet produced only one writer who has distinguished himself in the department of fiction--albeit he who did so was a giant therein--I mean John Bunyan.

And here I may well be allowed an unintended digression, as to whether Bunyan were really a Gipsy. In a previous chapter of this work, I, with little thought of Bunyan, narrated the fact that an intelligent tinker, and a full Gipsy, asked me last summer in London, if I thought that the Rommany were of the Ten Tribes of Israel? When John Bunyan tells us explicitly that he once asked his father whether he and his relatives were of the race of the Israelites--he having then never seen a Jew--and when he carefully informs his readers that his descent was of a low and inconsiderable generation, "my father's house being of that rank that is meanest and most despised of all the families of the land," there remains no rational doubt whatever that Bunyan was indeed a Rom of the Rommany. "*Applico*" of which, as my own special and particular Gipsy is wont to say--it is worth noting that the magician Shakespeare, who knew everything, showed himself superior to many modern dramatists in being aware that the tinkers of England had, not a peculiar cant, but a special *language*.

And now for the letters. One day Ward'engro of the K'allis's Gav, asked me to write him a letter to his daughter, in Rommany. So I began to write from his dictation. But being, like all his race, unused to literary labour, his lively imagination continually led him astray, and as I found amusement in his so doing, it proved to be an easy matter to induce him to wander off into scenes of gipsy life, which, however edifying they might be to my reader, would certainly not have the charm of novelty to the black-eyed lady to whom they were supposed to be addressed. However, as I read over from time to time to my Rommany chal what I had written, his delight in actually hearing his own words read from writing, partook of all the pride of successful authorship--it was, my dear sir, like your delight over your first proof sheet.

Well, this was the letter. A translation will be found following it.

THE PANNI GAV, *Dec*. 16, 1871.

MY KAMLI CHAVI,--Kushti bak! My cammoben to turo mush an' turo dadas an' besto bak. We've had wafri bak, my pen's been naflo this here cooricus, we're doin' very wafro and couldn't lel no wongur. Your dui pals are kairin kushto, prasturin 'bout the tem, bickinin covvas. {65} Your puro kako welled acai to his pen, and hatched trin divvus, and jawed avree like a puro jucko, and never del mandy a poshero.

Kek adusta nevvi. A rakli acai lelled a hora waver divvus from a waver rakli, and the one who nashered it pens: "Del it pauli a mandi and I wont dukker tute! Del it apre!" But the waver rakli penned "kek," and so they bitchered for the prastramengro. He lelled the juva to the wardo, and just before she welled odoi, she hatched her wast in her poachy, an' chiv it avree, and the prastramengro hatched it apre. So they bitchered her for shurabun.

(Here my Gipsy suggested that *stardo* or *staramangro* might be used for greater elegance, in place of shurabun.)

I've got kek gry and can't lel no wongur to kin kek. My kamli chavi, if you could bitch me a few bars it would be cammoben. I rikkers my covvas apre mi dumo kenna. I dicked my kako, waver divvus adree a lot o Rommany chals, saw a piin'. There was the juvas a koorin adoi and the mushis a koorin an' there was a boro chingaree, some with kali yakkas an' some with sherros chinned so the ratt jalled alay 'pre the drum. There was dui or trin bar to pessur in the sala for the graias an' mylas that got in pandamam (***pandapenn***).

Your pal's got a kushti gry that can jal alangus the drum kushto. L--- too's got a baro kushto gry. He jawed to the wellgooro, to the boro gav, with a poggobavescro gry an' a nokengro. You could a mored dovo gry an' kek penn'd a lav tute. I del it some ballovas to hatch his bavol and I bikened it for 9 bar, to a rye that you jins kushto. Lotti was at the wellgooro dukkerin the ranis. She lelled some kushti habben, an' her jellico was saw porder, when she dicked her mush and shelled. "Havacai! I've got some fine habben!" She penned to a rakli, "Pet your wonger adree turo wast an I'll dukker tute." An' she lelled a pash bar from the rani. She penned her: "You kaums a rye a longo duros. He's a kaulo and there's a waver rye, a pauno, that kaums you too, an' you'll soon lel a chinamangree. Tute'll rummorben before dui besh, an' be the dye of trin chavis.'

There was a gry jallin with a wardo langus the drum, an' I dicked a raklo, an' putsched (***pootched***) him. "How much wongur?" an' he pookered man'y "Desh bar;" I penned: "Is dovo, noko gry?" "Avali." Well, a Rommany chul del him desh bar for the gry an' bikined it for twelve bar to a boro rye. It was a fino kaulo gry with a boro herree, but had a naflo piro; it was the ***nearo*** piro an' was a dellemescro. He del it some hopium drab to hatch adoi, and tooled his solivengro upo the purgis.

At the paiass with the koshters a rye welled and Wantelo shelled avree: "Trin kosters for a horra, eighteen for a shekori!" An' the rye lelled a koshter an' we had pange collos for trin dozenos. The rye kaired paiass kushto and lelled pange cocoanuts, and lelled us to his wardo, and dell'd mandy trin currus of tatty panni, so that I was most matto. He was a kushti rye and his rani was as good as the rye.

There was a waver mush a playin, an' mandy penned: "Pen the kosh paulier, hatch 'em odoi, don't well adoorer or he'll lel saw the covvos! Chiv 'em pauli!" A chi rakkered the ryes an' got fifteen cullos from yeck. And no moro the divvus from your kaum pal,

M.

TRANSLATION.

THE WATER VILLAGE, ***Dec***. 16, 1871.

MY DEAR DAUGHTER,--Good luck! my love to your husband and your father, and best luck! We've had bad fortune, my sister has been sick this here week, we're doing very badly and could not get any money. Your two brothers are doing well, running about the country selling things. Your old uncle came to his sister and stayed three days, and went away like an old dog and never gave me a penny.

Nothing much new. A girl here took a watch the other day from another girl, and the one who lost it said: "Give it back to me and I won't hurt you." But the other girl said "No," and so they sent for the constable. He took the girl to the station (or carriage), and just before she got there she put her hand in her pocket and threw it away, and the policeman picked it up. So they sent her to prison.

I have no horse, and can't get any money to buy **none**. My dear daughter, if you could send me a few pounds it would be agreeable. I carry my **traps** on my back now. I saw my uncle the other day among a lot of Gipsies, all drinking. There were the women fighting there, and the men fighting, and there was a great **shindy**, some with black eyes, and some with heads cut so that the blood ran down on the road. There were two or three pounds to pay in the morning for the horses and asses that were in the pound.

Your brother has got a capital horse that can go along the road nicely. L---, too, has a large fine horse. He went to the fair in --- with a broken-winded horse and a glandered. You could have killed that horse and nobody said a word to you. I gave it some lard to stop his breathing, and I sold it for nine pound to a gentleman whom you know well.

Lotty was at the fair telling fortunes to the ladies. She got some excellent food, and her apron was quite full, when she saw her husband and cried out: "Come here! I've got some nice victuals!" She said to a girl: "Put you money in your hand and I'll tell you your fortune." And she took half a sovereign from the lady. She told her: "You love a gentleman who is far away. He is dark, and there is another gentleman, a fair-haired man that loves you, and you'll soon get a letter. You'll marry before two years, and be the mother of three children."

There was a horse going with a waggon along the road; and I saw a youth, and asked him, "How much money?" (for the horse), and he replied to me, "Ten pounds." I said, "Is that your horse?" "Yes." Well, a Gipsy gave him ten pounds for the horse, and sold it for twelve pounds to a great gentleman. It was a good black horse, with a (handsome) strong leg (literally large), but it had a bad foot; it was the *near* foot, and it was a kicker. He gave it some opium medicament to keep quiet (literally to stop there), and held his rein (*i.e.*, trotted him so as to show his pace, and conceal his faults) on the road.

At the cock-shy a gentleman came, and Wantelo hallooed out, "Three sticks for a penny, eighteen for a sixpence!" And the gentleman took a stick, and we had five shillings for three dozen throws! The gentleman played well, and got five cocoa-nuts, and took us to his carriage and gave me three glasses of brandy, so that I was almost drunk. He was a good gentleman, and his lady was as good as her husband.

There was another man playing; and I said, "Set the sticks more back, set 'em there; don't go further or he'll get all the things! Set 'em back!" A Gipsy girl talked to the gentlemen (*i.e.*, persuaded them to play), and got fifteen shillings from one. And no more to-day from your dear brother,

M.

* * * *

One thing in the foregoing letter is worth noting. Every remark or incident oc-curring in it is literally true--drawn from life--*pur et simple*. It is, indeed, almost the *resume* of the entire life of many poor Gipsies during the summer. And I may add that the language in which it is written, though not the "deep" or grammatical Gipsy, in which no English words occur--as for instance in the Lord's Prayer, as given by Mr Borrow in his appendix to the Gipsies in Spain {70}--is still really a fair specimen of the Rommany of the present day, which is spoken at races by cock-shysters and fortune-tellers.

The "Water Village," from which it is dated, is the generic term among Gipsies for all towns by the sea-side. The phrase *kushto* (or *kushti*), *bak*!--"good luck!" is after " *Sarishan*!" or "how are you?" the common greeting among Gipsies. The fight is from life and to the life; and the "two or three pounds to pay in the morning for the horses and asses that got impounded," indicates its magnitude. To have a beast in pound in consequence of a frolic, is a common disaster in Gipsy life.

During the dictation of the foregoing letter, my Gipsy paused at the word "broken-winded horse," when I asked him how he could stop the heavy breathing?

"With ballovas (or lard and starch)--long enough to sell it."

"But how would you sell a glandered horse?"

Here he described, with great ingenuity, the manner in which he would ***tool*** or manage the horse--an art in which Gipsies excel all the world over--and which, as Mr Borrow tells us, they call in Spain "***de pacuaro***," which is pure Persian.

"But that would not stop the running. How would you prevent that?"

"I don't know."

"Then I am a better graiengro than you, for I know a powder, and with a penny's worth of it I could stop the glanders in the worst case, long enough to sell the horse. I once knew an old horse-dealer who paid sixty pounds for a ***nokengro*** (a glandered horse) which had been powdered in this way."

The Gipsy listened to me in great admiration. About a week afterwards I heard he had spoken of me as follows:--

"Don't talk about knowing. My rye knows more than anybody. He can cheat any man in England selling him a glandered horse."

Had this letter been strictly confined to the limits originally intended, it would have spoken only of the sufferings of the family, the want of money, and possibly, the acquisition of a new horse by the brother. In this case it bears a decided family-likeness to the following letter in the German-Gipsy dialect, which originally appeared in a book entitled, ***Beytrag zur Rottwellischen Grammatik***, ***oder Worterbuch von der Zigeuner Spracke***, Leipzig 1755, and which was republished by Dr A. F. Pott in his stupendous work, ***Die Zigeuner in Europa und Asien***. Halle, 1844.

GERMAN GIPSY.

MIRI KOMLI ROMNI,--Ertiewium Francfurtter wium te gajum apro Newoforo. Apro drum ne his mange mishdo. Mare manush tschingerwenes ketteni. Tschiel his te midschach wettra. Tschawe wele naswele. Dowa ker, kai me gaijam medre gazdias tele; mare ziga t'o terno kalbo nahsle penge. O flachso te hanfa te wulla te schwigarizakri te stifftshakri ho spinderde gotshias nina. Lopennawa, wium ke tshorero te wiam hallauter nange Denkerdum tschingerwam mangi kasht te mre wastiengri butin, oder hunte di kaw te kinnaw tschommoni pre te bikkewaw pale, te de denkerwaw te ehrnahrwaw man kiacke. Me bium kiacke kuremangrender pene aper mande, buten tschingerde buten trinen marde te man, tshimaster apri butin tshidde. O bolloben te rackel tutt andre sawe kolester, kai me wium adre te me tshawa tiro rum shin andro meraben.

TRANSLATION.

MY DEAR WIFE,--Before I came to Frankfort I went to Neustadt. On the way it did not go well with me. Our men quarrelled together. It was cold and wet weather. The children were ill. That house into which we had gone burnt down; our kid and the young calf run away. The flax and hemp and wool [which] the sister-in-law and step-daughter spun are also burned. In short, I say I became so poor that we all went naked. I thought of cutting wood and working by hand, or I should go into business and sell something. I think I will make my living so. I was so treated by the soldiers. They fell on us, wounded many, three they killed, and I was taken to prison to work for life. Heaven preserve you in all things from that into which I have fallen, and I remain thy husband unto death.

* * * *

It is the same sad story in all, wretchedness, poverty, losses, and hunger. In the English letter there was a *chingari*--a shindy; in the German they have a *tshinger*, which is nearly the same word, and means the same. It may be remarked as curious that the word *meraben* at the end of the letter, meaning death, is used by English Gipsies to signify life as well.

> "Dick at the gorgios,
> The gorgios round mandy;
> Trying to take my meripon,
> My meripon away."

The third letter is also in the German-Gipsy dialect, and requires a little explanation. Once a man named Charles Augustus was arrested as a beggar and suspected Gipsy, and brought before Mr Richard Liebich, who appears to have been nothing less in the total than the *Furstlich Reuss- Plauenschem Criminalrathe und Vor-*

stande des Furstlichen Criminalgerichts zu Lobenstein--in fact, a rather lofty local magistrate. Before this terrible title Charles appeared, and swore stoutly that he was no more a Rommany chal than he was one of the Apostles--for be it remembered, reader, that in Germany at the present day, the mere fact of being a Gipsy is still treated as a crime. Suddenly the judge attacked him with the words--" ***Tu hal rom, me hom, rakker tschatschopenn***!"--"Thou art a Gipsy, I am a Gipsy, speak the truth." And Charles, looking up in amazement and seeing the black hair and brown face of the judge, verily believed that he was of the blood of Dom. So crossing his arms on his breast in true Oriental style, he salaamed deeply, and in a submissive voice said--" ***Me hom rom***"--" *I am a* Gipsy."

The judge did not abuse the confidence gained by his little trick, since he appears to have taken Charles under his wing, employed him in small jobs (in America we should say ***chores***, but the word would be frightfully significant, if applied to a Gipsy), {75} and finally dismissed him. And Charles replied Rommanesquely, by asking for something. His application was as follows:--

GERMAN GIPSY.

"LICHTENBERG ANE DESCHE OCHDADO, *Januar* 1859.

"LADSCHO BARO RAI,--Me hunde dschinawe duge gole dui trin Lawinser mire zelle gowe, har geas mange an demaro foro de demare Birengerenser. Har weum me stildo gage lean demare Birengere mr lowe dele, de har weum biro gage lean jon man dran o stilibin bri, de mangum me mr lowe lender, gai deum dele. Jon pendin len wellen geg mander. Gai me deum miro lowe lende, naste pennene jon gar wawer. Brinscherdo lowe hi an i Gissig, o baro godder lolo paro, trin Chairingere de jeg dschildo gotter sinagro lowe. Man weas mr lowe gar gobe dschanel o Baro Dewel ani Bolebin. Miro baaro bargerbin vaschge demare Ladschebin bennawe. O baro Dewel de pleisserwel de maro ladscho sii i pure sasde Tschiwaha demende demaro zelo Beero. De hadzin e Birengere miro lowe, dale mangawa me len de bidschin jon mire lowe gadder o foro Naile abbi Bidschebasger wurtum sikk. Gai me dschingerdum ab demende, hi gar dschadscho, gai miri romni hass mando, gowe hi dschadscho. Obaaro Dewel de bleiserwel de mange de menge demaro Ladscho Sii. Miero Bargerbin. De me dschawe demaro gandelo Waleddo.

CHARLES AUGUSTIN."

TRANSLATION.

"LICHTENBERG, *January* 18, 1859.

"GOOD GREAT SIR,--I must write to you with these two or three words my whole business (**gowe**, English Gipsy **covvo**, literally 'thing,') how it happened to me in your town, by your servants (literally 'footmen'). When I was arrested, your servants took my money away, and when I was freed they took me out of prison. I asked my money of them which I had given up. They said they had got none from me. That I gave them my money they cannot deny. The said (literally, known) money is in a purse, a great piece, red (and) old, three kreutzers, and a yellow piece of good-for- nothing money. I did not get my money, as the great God in heaven knows. My great thanks for your goodness, I say. The great God reward your good heart with long healthy life, you and your whole family. And if your servants find my money, I beg they will send it to the town Naila, by the post at once. That I cursed you is not true; that my wife was drunk is true. The great God reward your good heart. My thanks. And I remain, your obedient servant,

CHARLES AUGUSTIN."

Those who attempt to read this letter in the original, should be informed that German Gipsy is, as compared to the English or Spanish dialects, almost a perfect language; in fact, Pott has by incredible industry, actually restored it to its primitive complete form; and its orthography is now settled. Against this orthography poor Charles Augustin sins sadly, and yet it may be doubted whether many English tramps and beggars could write a better letter.

The especial Gipsy characteristic in this letter is the constant use of the name of God, and the pious profusion of blessings. "She's the **blessing-est** old woman I ever came across," was very well said of an old Rommany dame in England. And yet these well-wishings are not always insincere, and they are earnest enough when uttered in Gipsy.

CHAPTER VI. GIPSY WORDS WHICH HAVE PASSED INTO ENGLISH SLANG.

Jockey.--Tool.--Cove or Covey.--Hook, Hookey, and Walker, Hocus, Hanky- Panky, and Hocus-Pocus.--Shindy.--Row.--Chivvy.--Bunged Eye.--Shavers.-- Clichy.--Caliban.--A Rum 'un.--Pal.--Trash.--Cadger.--Cad.--Bosh.--Bats.-- Chee-chee.--The Cheese.--Chiv Fencer.--Cooter.--Gorger.--Dick.--Dook.-- Tanner.--Drum.--Gibberish.--Ken.--Lil.--Loure.--Loafer.--Maunder.--Moke.-- Parny.--Posh.--Queer. Raclan.--Bivvy.--Rigs.--Moll.--Distarabin.--Tiny.-- Toffer.--Tool.--Punch.--Wardo.--Voker (one of Mr Hotten's Gipsy words).-- Welcher.--Yack.--Lushy.--A Mull.--Pross.--Toshers.--Up to Trap.--Barney.-- Beebee.--Cull, Culley.--Jomer.--Bloke.--Duffer.--Niggling.--Mug.-- Bamboozle, Slang, and Bite.--Rules to be observed in determining the Etymology of Gipsy Words.

Though the language of the Gipsies has been kept a great secret for centuries, still a few words have in England oozed out here and there from some unguarded crevice, and become a portion of our tongue. There is, it must be admitted, a great difficulty in tracing, with anything like accuracy, the real origin or identity of such expressions. Some of them came into English centuries ago, and during that time great changes have taken place in Rommany. At least one-third of the words now used by Scottish Gipsies are unintelligible to their English brothers. To satisfy myself on this point, I have examined an intelligent English Gipsy on the Scottish Gipsy vocabularies in Mr Simpson's work, and found it was as I anticipated; a statement which will not appear incredible when it is remembered, that even the Rommany of Yetholm have a dialect marked and distinct from that of other Scotch Gipsies. As for England, numbers of the words collected by William

Marsden, and Jacob Bryant, in 1784-5, Dr Bright in 1817, and by Harriott in 1830, are not known at the present day to any Gipsies whom I have met. Again, it should be remembered that the pronunciation of Rommany differs widely with individuals; thus the word which is given as *cumbo*, a hill, by Bryant, I have heard very distinctly pronounced *choomure*.

I believe that to Mr Borrow is due the discovery that the word JOCKEY is of Gipsy origin, and derived from *chuckni*, which means a whip. For nothing is more clearly established than that the jockey-whip was the original term in which this word first made its appearance on the turf, and that the *chuckni* was a peculiar form of whip, very long and heavy, first used by the Gipsies. "Jockeyism," says Mr Borrow, "properly means *the management of a whip*, and the word jockey is neither more nor less than the term, slightly modified, by which they designate the formidable whips which they usually carry, and which are at present in general use among horse-traffickers, under the title of jockey-whips." In Hungary and Germany the word occurs as *tschuckini* or *chookni*, and *tschupni*.

Many of my readers are doubtless familiar with the word to TOOL as applied to dexterously managing the reins and driving horses. 'To tool the horses down the road,' is indeed rather a fine word of its class, being as much used in certain clubs as in stables, and often denotes stylish and gentlemanly driving. And the term is without the slightest modification, either of pronunciation or meaning, directly and simply Gipsy, and is used by Gipsies in the same way. It has, however, in Rommany, as a primitive meaning--to hold, or to take. Thus I have heard of a feeble old fellow that "he could not tool himself togetherus"--for which last word, by the way, *kettenus* might have been more correctly substituted.

COVE is not an elegant, though a very old, word, but it is well known, and I have no doubt as to its having come from the Gipsy. In Rommany, all the world over, *cova* means "a thing," but it is almost indefinite in its applicability. "It is," says Pott, "a general helper on all occasions; is used as substantive and adjective, and has a far wider scope than the Latin *res*." Thus *covo* may mean "that man;" *covi*, "that woman;" and *covo* or *cuvvo*, as it very often does in English, "that, there." It sometimes appears in the word *acovat*, or *this*. There is no expression more frequent in a Gipsy's mouth, and it is precisely the one which would be probably overheard by "Gorgios" and applied to persons. I believe that it first made its appearance in English slang as *covey*, and was then pronounced *cuvvy*, being subsequently abbreviated into cove.

Quite a little family of words has come into English from the Rommany, *Hocben*, *huckaben*, *hokkeny*, or *hooker*, all meaning a lie, or to lie, deception and *humbug*. Mr Borrow shows us that *hocus*, to "bewitch" liquor with an opiate, and *hoax*, are probably Rommany from this root, and I have no doubt that the expression, "Yes, with a *hook*," meaning "it is false," comes from the same. The well-known "Hookey" who corresponds so closely with his untruthful and disreputable pal "Walker," is decidedly of the streets--gipsy. In German Gipsy we find *chochavav* and *hochewawa*, and in Roumanian Gipsy *kokao*--a lie. Hanky-panky and Hocus-pocus are each one half almost pure Hindustani. {81}

A SHINDY approaches so nearly in sound to the Gipsy word *chingaree*, which means precisely the same thing, that the suggestion is at least worth consideration. And it also greatly resembles *chindi*, which may be translated as "cutting up," and also quarrel. "To cut up shindies" was the first form in which this extraordinary word reached the public. In the original Gipsy tongue the word to quarrel is *chinger-av*, meaning also (Pott, *Zigeuner*, p. 209) to cut, hew, and fight, while to cut is *chinav*. "Cutting up" is, if the reader reflects, a very unmeaning word as applied to outrageous or noisy pranks; but in Gipsy, whether English, German, or Oriental, it is perfectly sensible and logical, involving the idea of quarrelling, separating, dividing, cutting, and stabbing. What, indeed, could be more absurd than the expression "cutting up shines," unless we attribute to *shine* its legitimate Gipsy meaning of *a piece cut off*, and its cognate meaning, a noise?

I can see but little reason for saying that a man *cut away* or that he *shinned* it, for run away, unless we have recourse to Gipsy, though I only offer this as a mere suggestion.

"Applico" to shindy we have the word ROW, meaning nearly the same thing and as nearly Gipsy in every respect as can be. It is in Gipsy at the present day in England, correctly, *rov*, or *roven*--to cry--but *v* and *w* are so frequently transposed that we may consider them as the same letter. *Raw* or *me rauaw*, "I howl" or "cry," is German Gipsy. *Rowan* is given by Pott as equivalent to the Latin *ulu-*

latus, which constituted a very respectable *row* as regards mere noise. "Rowdy" comes from "row" and both are very good Gipsy in their origin. In Hindustani **Rao mut** is "don't cry!"

CHIVVY is a common English vulgar word, meaning to goad, drive, vex, hunt, or throw as it were here and there. It is purely Gipsy, and seems to have more than one root. *Chiv*, *chib*, or *chipe*, in Rommany, mean a tongue, inferring scolding, and *chiv* anything sharp-pointed, as for instance a dagger, or goad or knife. But the old Gipsy word *chiv-av* among its numerous meanings has exactly that of casting, throwing, pitching, and driving. To *chiv* in English Gipsy means as much and more than to *fix* in America, in fact, it is applied to almost any kind of action.

It may be remarked in this connection, that in German or continental Gipsy, which represents the English in a great measure as it once was, and which is far more perfect as to grammar, we find different words, which in English have become blended into one. Thus, *chib* or *chiv*, a tongue, and **tschiwawa** (or *chiv*-ava), to lay, place, lean, sow, sink, set upright, move, harness, cover up, are united in England into *chiv*, which embraces the whole. "*Chiv it apre*" may be applied to throwing anything, to covering it up, to lifting it, to setting it, to pushing it, to circulating, and in fact to a very great number of similar verbs.

There is, I think, no rational connection between the BUNG of a barrel and an eye which has been closed by a blow. One might as well get the simile from a knot in a tree or a cork in a flask. But when we reflect on the constant mingling of Gipsies with prizefighters, it is almost evident that the word BONGO may have been the origin of it. A **bongo yakko** or **yak**, means a distorted, crooked, or, in fact, a bunged eye. It also means lame, crooked, or sinister, and by a very singular figure of speech, **Bongo Tem** or the Crooked Land is the name for hell. {83}

SHAVERS, as a quaint nick-name for children, is possibly inexplicable, unless we resort to Gipsy, where we find it used as directly as possible. **Chavo** is the Rommany word for child all the world over, and the English term **chavies**, in Scottish Gipsy **shavies**, or shavers, leaves us but little room for doubt. I am not aware to what extent the term "little shavers" is applied to children in England, but in America it is as common as any cant word can be.

I do not know the origin of the French word CLICHY, as applied to the noted prison of that name, but it is perhaps not undeserving the comment that in Continental Gipsy it means a key and a bolt.

I have been struck with the fact that CALIBAN, the monster in "The Tempest," by Shakespeare, has an appellation which literally signifies blackness in Gipsy. In fact, this very word, or Cauliban, is given in one of the Gipsy vocabularies for "black." Kaulopen or Kauloben would, however, be more correct.

"A regular RUM 'un" was the form in which the application of the word "rum" to strange, difficult, or distinguished, was first introduced to the British public. This, I honestly believe (as Mr Borrow indicates), came from *Rum* or *Rom*, a Gipsy. It is a peculiar word, and all of its peculiarities might well be assumed by the sporting Gipsy, who is always, in his way, a character, gifted with an indescribable self-confidence, as are all "horsey" men characters, "sports" and boxers, which enables them to keep to perfection the German eleventh commandment, "Thou shall not let thyself be *bluffed*!"-- *i.e* ., abashed.

PAL is a common cant word for brother or friend, and it is purely Gipsy, having come directly from that language, without the slightest change. On the Continent it is *prala*, or *pral*. In England it sometimes takes the form "*pel*."

TRASH is derived by Mr Wedgwood (Dictionary of English Etymology, 1872) from the old word *trousse*, signifying the clipping of trees. But in old Gipsy or in the German Gipsy of the present day, as in the Turkish Rommany, it means so directly "fear, mental weakness and worthlessness," that it may possibly have had a Rommany origin. Terror in Gipsy is *trash*, while thirst is *trush*, and both are to be found in the Hindustani. *Tras*, which means *thirst* and *alarm* or *terror*.

It should be observed that in no instance can these Gipsy words have been borrowed from English slang. They are all to be found in German Gipsy, which is in its turn identical with the Rommany language of India--of the Nats, Bhazeghurs, Doms, Multanee or Banjoree, as I find the primitive wandering Gipsies termed by different writers.

I am aware that the word CAD was applied to the conductor of an omnibus, or to a non-student at Universities, before it became a synonym for vulgar fellow, yet I believe that it was abbreviated from cadger, and that this is simply the Gipsy word Gorgio, which often means a man in the abstract. I have seen this word printed as gorger in English slang. CODGER, which is common, is applied, as Gipsies use the term Gorgio, contemptuously, and it sounds still more like it.

BOSH, signifying nothing, or in fact empty humbug, is generally credited to the Turkish language, but I can see no reason for going to the Turks for what the Gipsies at home already had, in all probability, from the same Persian source, or else from the Sanskrit. With the Gipsies, *bosh* is a fiddle, music, noise, barking, and very often an idle sound or nonsense. "Stop your bosherin," or "your bosh," is what they would term *flickin lav*, or current phrase.

"BATS," a low term for a pair of boots, especially bad ones, is, I think, from the Gipsy and Hindustani *pat*, a foot, generally called, however, by the Rommany in England, Tom Pats. "To pad the hoof," and "to stand pad "--the latter phrase meaning to stand upright, or to stand and beg, are probably derived from *pat*. It should be borne in mind that Gipsies, in all countries, are in the habit of changing certain letters, so that *p* and *b*, like *l* and *n*, or *k* and *g* hard, may often be regarded as identical.

"CHEE-CHEE," "be silent!" or "fie," is termed "Anglo-Indian," by the author of the Slang Dictionary, but we need not go to India of the present day for a term which is familiar to every Gipsy and "traveller" in England, and which, as Mr Simson discovered long ago, is an excellent "spell" to discourage the advances of thimble-riggers and similar gentry, at fairs, or in public places.

CHEESE, or "THE CHEESE," meaning that anything is pre-eminent or superior; in fact, "the thing," is supposed by many to be of gipsy origin because Gipsies use it, and it is to be found as "chiz" in Hindustani, in which language it means a thing. Gipsies do not, however, seem to regard it themselves, as *tacho* or true Rommanis, despite this testimony, and I am inclined to think that it partly originated in some wag's perversion of the French word *chose*.

In London, a man who sells cutlery in the streets is called a CHIVE FENCER, a term evidently derived from the Gipsy *chiv*, a sharp-pointed instrument or knife. A knife is also called a *chiv* by the lowest class all over England.

COUTER or COOTER is a common English slang term for a guinea. It was not necessary for the author of the Slang Dictionary to go to the banks of the Danube for the origin of a word which is in the mouths of all English Gipsies, and which was brought to England by their ancestors. A sovereign, a pound, in Gipsy, is a *bar*.

A GORGER, meaning a gentleman, or well-dressed man, and in theatrical parlance, a manager, is derived by the author of the Slang Dictionary--absurdly enough, it must be confessed--from "gorgeous,"--a word with which it has no more in common than with gouges or chisels. A gorger or gorgio--the two are often confounded--is the common Gipsy word for one who is not Gipsy, and very often means with them a *rye* or gentleman, and indeed any man whatever. Actors sometimes call a fellow- performer a *cully-gorger*.

DICK, an English slang word for sight, or seeing, is purely Gipsy in its origin, and in common use by Rommanis over all the world.

DOOK, to tell fortunes, and DOOKING, fortune-telling, are derived by the writer last cited, correctly enough, from the Gipsy *dukkerin*,--a fact which I specify, since it is one of the very rare instances in which he has not blundered when commenting on Rommany words, or other persons' works.

Mr Borrow has told us that a TANNER or sixpence, sometimes called a Downer, owes its pseudonym to the Gipsy word *tawno* or *tano*, meaning "little"--the sixpence being the little coin as compared with a shilling.

DRUM or DROM, is the common English Gipsy word for a road. In English slang it is applied, not only to highways, but also to houses.

If the word GIBBERISH was, as has been asserted, first applied to the language of the Gipsies, it may have been derived either from "Gip," the nickname for Gipsy, with *ish* or *rish* appended as in Engl- *ish*, I- *rish*, or from the Rommany word *Jib* signifying a language.

KEN, a low term for a house, is possibly of Gipsy origin. The common word in every Rommany dialect for a house is, however, neither ken nor khan, but *Ker*.

LIL, a book, a letter, has passed from the Gipsies to the low "Gorgios," though it is not a very common word. In Rommany it can be *correctly* applied only to a letter or a piece of paper, which is written on, though English Gipsies call all books by this name, and often speak of a letter as a *Chinamangri*.

LOUR or LOWR, and LOAVER, are all vulgar terms for money, and combine two Gipsy words, the one *lovo* or *lovey*, and the other *loure*, to steal. The reason for the combination or confusion is obvious. The author of the Slang Dictionary, in order to explain this word, goes as usual to the Wallachian Gipsies, for what he might have learned from the first tinker in the streets of London. I should remark on the word loure, that Mr Borrow has shown its original identity with *loot*, the Hindustani for plunder or booty.

I believe that the American word loafer owes something to this Gipsy root, as well as to the German *laufer* (*landlaufer*), and Mexican Spanish *galeofar*, and for this reason, that when the term first began to be popular in 1834 or 1835, I can distinctly remember that it meant to *pilfer*. Such, at least, is my earliest recollection, and of hearing school boys ask one another in jest, of their acquisitions or gifts, "Where did you loaf that from?" A petty pilferer was a loafer, but in a very short time all of the tribe of loungers in the sun, and disreputable pickers up of unconsidered trifles, now known as bummers, were called loafers. On this point my memory is positive, and I call attention to it, since the word in question has been the subject of much conjecture in America.

It is a very curious fact, that while the word *loot* is unquestionably Anglo-Indian, and only a recent importation into our English "slanguage," it has always been at the same time English-Gipsy, although it never rose to the surface.

MAUNDER, to stroll about and beg, has been derived from *Mand*, the Anglo-Saxon for a basket, but is quite as likely to have come from Maunder, the Gipsy for "to beg." Mumper, a beggar, is also from the same source.

MOKE, a donkey, is *said* to be Gipsy, by Mr Hotten, but Gipsies themselves do not use the word, nor does it belong to their usual language. The proper Rommany word for an ass is *myla*.

PARNY, a vulgar word for rain, is supposed to have come into England from the "Anglo-Indian" source, but it is more likely that it was derived from the Gipsy *panni* or water. "Brandy pawnee" is undoubtedly an Anglo-Indian word, but it is used by a very different class of people from those who know the meaning of *Parny*.

POSH, which has found its way into vulgar popularity, as a term for small coins, and sometimes for money in general, is the diminutive of the Gipsy word *pashero* or *poshero*, a half-penny, from *pash* a half, and *haura* or *harra*, a penny.

QUEER, meaning across, cross, contradictory, or bad, is "supposed" to be the German word *quer*, introduced by the Gipsies. In their own language *atut* means across or against, though to *curry* (German and Turkish Gipsy *kurava*), has some of the slang meaning attributed to *queer*. An English rogue will say, "to shove the queer," meaning to pass counterfeit money, while the Gipsy term would be to *chiv wafri lovvo*, or *lovey*.

"RAGLAN, a married woman, originally *Gipsy*, but now a term with English tramps" (*The Slang Dictionary*, *London* 1865). In Gipsy, *raklo* is a youth or boy, and *rakli*, a girl; Arabic, *ragol*, a man. I am informed, on good authority, that these words are known in India, though I cannot find them in dictionaries. They are possibly transposed from *Lurka* a youth and *lurki* a girl, such transpositions being common among the lowest classes in India.

RUMMY or RUMY, as applied to women, is simply the Gipsy word *romi*, a contraction of *romni*, a wife; the husband being her *rom*.

BIVVY for beer, has been derived from the Italian *bevere*, but it is probably Gipsy, since in the old form of the latter language, Biava or Piava, means to drink. To *pivit*, is still known among English Gipsies.

RIGS--running one's rigs is said to be Gipsy, but the only meaning of *rig*, so far as I am able to ascertain in Rommany, is *a side* or *an edge*. It is, however, possible that one's *side* may in earlier times have been equivalent to "face, or encounter." To *rikker* or *rigger* in Gipsy, is to carry anything.

MOLL, a female companion, is probably merely the nickname for Mary, but it is worth observing, that *Mal* in old Gipsy, or in German Gipsy, means an associate, and Mahar a wife, in Hindustani.

STASH, to be quiet, to stop, is, I think, a variation of the common Gipsy word hatch, which means precisely the same thing, and is derived from the older word *atchava*.

STURABAN, a prison, is purely Gipsy. Mr Hotten says it is from the Gipsy *dis-tarabin*, but there is no such word beginning with *dis*, in the English Rommany dialect. In German Gipsy a prison is called *stillapenn*.

TINY or TEENY has been derived from the Gipsy *tano*, meaning "little."

TOFFER, a woman who is well dressed in new clean clothes, probably gets the name from the Gipsy *tove*, to wash (German Gipsy *Tovava*). She is, so to speak, freshly washed. To this class belong Toff, a dandy; *Tofficky*, dressy or gay, and *Toft*, a dandy or swell.

TOOL as applied to stealing, picking pockets, and burglary, is, like *tool*, to drive with the reins; derived beyond doubt from the Gipsy word *tool*, to take or hold. In all the Continental Rommany dialects it is *Tulliwawa*.

PUNCH, it is generally thought, is Anglo-Indian, derived directly from the Hindustani *Pantch* or five, from the five ingredients which enter into its composition, but it may have partially got its name from some sporting Gipsy in whose language the word for *five* is the same as in Sanskrit. There have been thousands of "swell" Rommany chals who have moved in sporting circles of a higher class than they are to be found in at the present day.

"VARDO formerly was *Old Cant* for a waggon" (*The Slang Dictionary*). It may be added that it is pure Gipsy, and is still known at the present day to every Rom in England. In Turkish Gipsy, *Vordon* means a vehicle, in German Gipsy, *Wortin*.

"Can you VOKER Rommany?" is given by Mr Hotten as meaning "Can you speak Gipsy,"--but there is no such word in Rommany as *voker*. He probably meant "Can you *rakker*"--pronounced very often *Roker*. Continental Gipsy *Rakkervava*. Mr Hotten derives it from the Latin *Vocare*!

I do not know the origin of WELCHER, a betting cheat, but it is worthy of remark that in old Gipsy a *Walshdo* or Welsher meant a Frenchman (from the German Walsch) or any foreigner of the Latin races.

YACK, a watch, probably received its name from the Gipsy *Yak* an eye, in the old times when watches were called bull's eyes.

LUSHY, to be tipsy, and LUSH, are attributed for their origin to the name of Lushington, a once well-known London brewer, but when we find *Losho* and *Loshano* in a Gipsy dialect, meaning jolly, from such a Sanskrit root as *Lush*; as Paspati derives it, there seems to be some ground for supposing the words to be purely Rommany. Dr Johnson said of lush that it was "opposite to pale," and this curiously enough shows its first source, whether as a "slang" word or as indicative of colour, since one of its early Sanskrit meanings is *light* or *radiance*. This identity of the so regarded vulgar and the refined, continually confronts us in studying Rommany.

"To make a MULL of anything," meaning thereby to spoil or confuse it, if it be derived, as is said, from the Gipsy, must have come from **Mullo** meaning **dead**, and the Sanskrit **Mara**. There is, however, no such Gipsy word as mull, in the sense of entangling or spoiling.

PROSS is a theatrical slang word, meaning to instruct and train a tyro. As there are several stage words of manifest Gipsy origin, I am inclined to derive this from the old Gipsy **Priss**, to read. In English Gipsy **Prasser** or **Pross** means to ridicule or scorn. Something of this is implied in the slang word **Pross**, since it also means "to sponge upon a comrade," &c., "for drink."

TOSHERS are in English low language, "men who steal copper from ship's bottoms." I cannot form any direct connection between this word and any in English Gipsy, but it is curious that in Turkish Gipsy **Tasi** is a cup, and in Turkish Persian it means, according to Paspati, a copper basin used in the baths. It is as characteristic of English Gipsy as of any of its cognate dialects, that we often find lurking in it the most remarkable Oriental fragments, which cannot be directly traced through the regular line of transmission.

UP TO TRAP means, in common slang, intelligent. It is worth observing, that in Gipsy, **drab** or **trap** (which words were pronounced alike by the first Gipsies who came from Germany to England), is used for medicine or poison, and the employment of the latter is regarded, even at the present, as the greatest Rommany secret. Indeed, it is only a few days since a Gipsy said to me, "If you know **drab**, you're up to everything; for there's nothing goes above that." With **drab** the Gipsy secures game, fish, pigs, and poultry; he quiets kicking horses until they can be sold; and last, not least, kills or catches rats and mice. As with the Indians of North America, **medicine**--whether to kill or cure--is to the Gipsy the art of arts, and those who affect a knowledge of it are always regarded as the most intelligent. It is, however, remarkable, that the Gipsy, though he lives in fields and woods, is, all the world over, far inferior to the American Indian as regards a knowledge of the properties of herbs or minerals. One may pick the first fifty plants which he sees in the woods, and show them to the first Indian whom he meets, with the absolute certainty that the latter will give him a name for every one, and describe in detail their qualities and their use as remedies. The Gipsy seldom has a name for anything of the kind. The country people in America, and even the farmers' boys, have probably inherited by tradition much of this knowledge from the aborigines.

BARNEY, a mob or crowd, may be derived from the Gipsy *baro*, great or many, which sometimes takes the form of *barno* or *barni*, and which suggests the Hindustani Bahrna "to increase, proceed, to gain, to be promoted;" and Bharna, "to fill, to satisfy, to be filled, &c."--(Brice's "Hindustani and English Dictionary." London, Trubner & Co., 1864).

BEEBEE, which the author of the Slang Dictionary declares means a lady, and is "Anglo-Indian," is in general use among English Gipsies for aunt. It is also a respectful form of address to any middle-aged woman, among friends.

CULL or CULLY, meaning a man or boy, in Old English cant, is certainly of Gipsy origin. *Chulai* signifies man in Spanish Gipsy (Borrow), and *Khulai* a gentleman, according to Paspati; in Turkish Rommany--a distinction which the word *cully* often preserves in England, even when used in a derogatory sense, as of a dupe.

JOMER, a sweetheart or female favourite, has probably some connection in derivation with choomer, a kiss, in Gipsy.

BLOKE, a common coarse word for a man, may be of Gipsy origin; since, as the author of the Slang Dictionary declares, it may be found in Hindustani, as Loke. "*Lok*, people, a world, region."--("Brice's Hind. Dictionary.") *Bala' lok*, a gentleman.

A DUFFER, which is an old English cant term, expressive of contempt for a man, may be derived from the Gipsy *Adovo*, "that," "that man," or "that fellow there." *Adovo* is frequently pronounced almost like "a duffer," or "*a duvva*."

NIGGLING, which means idling, wasting time, doing anything slowly, may be derived from some other Indo-European source, but in English Gipsy it means to go slowly, "to potter along," and in fact it is the same as the English word. That it is pure old Rommany appears from the fact that it is to be found as *Niglavava* in Turkish Gipsy, meaning "I go," which is also found in *Nikliovava* and *Nikavava*, which are in turn probably derived from the Hindustani *Nikalna*, "To issue, to go forth or out," &c. (Brice, Hind. Dic.) *Niggle* is one of the English Gipsy words which are used in the East, but which I have not been able to find in the German Rommany, proving that here, as in other countries, certain old forms have been preserved, though they have been lost where the vocabulary is far more copious, and the grammar much more perfect.

MUG, a face, is derived by Mr Wedgwood from the Italian MOCCA, a mocking or apish mouth (Dictionary of English Etymology), but in English Gipsy we have not only *mui*, meaning the face, but the *older* forms from which the English word was probably taken, such as Mak'h (Paspati), and finally the Hindustani *Mook* and the Sanskrit *Mukha*, mouth or face (Shakespeare, Hind. Dic., p. 745). In all cases where a word is so "slangy" as mug, it seems more likely that it should have been derived from Rommany than from Italian, since it is only within a few years that any considerable number of the words of the latter language was imparted to the lower classes of London.

BAMBOOZLE, BITE, and SLANG are all declared by the author of the Slang Dictionary to be Gipsy, but, with the exception of the last word, I am unable to verify their Rommany origin. Bambhorna does indeed mean in Hindustani (Brice), "to bite or to worry," and bamboo-bakshish to deceive by paying with a whipping, while *swang*, as signifying mimicking, acting, disguise and sham, whether of words or deeds, very curiously conveys the spirit of the word slang. As for *bite* I almost hesitate to suggest the possibility of a connection between it and *Bidorna*, to laugh at. I offer not only these three suggested derivations, but also most of the others, with every reservation. For many of these words, as for instance *bite*, etymologists have already suggested far more plausible and more probable derivations, and if I have found a place for Rommany "roots," it is simply because what is the most plausible, and apparently the most probable, is not always the true origin. But as I firmly believe that there is much more Gipsy in English, especially in English slang and cant, than the world is aware of, I think it advisable to suggest what I can, leaving to abler philologists the task of testing its value.

Writers on such subjects err, almost without an exception, in insisting on one accurately defined and singly derived source for every word, when perhaps three or four have combined to form it. The habits of thought and methods of study followed by philologists render them especially open to this charge. They wish to establish every form as symmetrical and mathematical, where nature has been freakish and bizarre. Some years ago when I published certain poems in the broken English spoken by Germans, an American philologist, named Haldemann, demonstrated to his own satisfaction that the language which I had put into Hans Breitmann's mouth was inaccurate, because I had not reduced it to an uniform dialect, making the same word the same in spelling and pronunciation on all occasions, when the most accurate observation had convinced me, as it must any one, that those who have only partially learned a language continually vary their methods of uttering its words.

That some words have come from one source and been aided by another, is continually apparent in English Gipsy, as for instance in the word for reins, "guiders," which, until the Rommany reached England, was voidas. In this instance the resemblance in sound between the words undoubtedly conduced to an union. Gibberish may have come from the Gipsy, and at the same time owe something to *gabble*, *jabber*, and the old Norse or Icelandic *gifra*. *Lush* may owe something to Mr Lushington, something to the earlier English *lush*, or rosy, and something to the Gipsy and Sanskrit. It is not at all unlikely that the word *codger* owes, through *cadger*, a part of its being to *kid*, a basket, as Mr Halliwell suggests (Dictionary of Archaic and Provincial Words, 1852), and yet come quite as directly from *gorger* or *gorgio*. "The cheese" probably has the Gipsy-Hidustani *chiz* for a father, and the French *chose* for a mother, while both originally sprung thousands of years ago in the great parting of the Aryan nations, to be united after so long a separation in a distant island in the far northern seas.

The etymologist who hesitates to adopt this principle of joint sources of derivation, will find abundant instances of something very like it in many English Gipsy words themselves, which, as belonging to a language in extreme decay, have been formed directly from different, but somewhat similarly sounding, words, in the parent German or Eastern Rommany. Thus, *schukker*, pretty; *bi-shukker*, slow; *tschukko*, dry, and *tschororanes*, secretly, have in England all united in *shukar*, which expresses all of their meanings.

CHAPTER VII. PROVERBS AND CHANCE PHRASES.

An Old Gipsy Proverb--Common Proverbs in Gipsy Dress--Quaint Sayings--Characteristic Rommany Picture-Phrases.

Every race has not only its peculiar proverbs, sayings, and catch-words, but also idiomatic phrases which constitute a characteristic chiaroscuro, if not colour. The Gipsies in England have of course borrowed much from the Gorgios, but now and then something of their own appears. In illustration of all this, I give the following expressions noted down from Gipsy conversation:--

Tacho like my dad. True like my father.

Kushto like my dad. Good like my father.

This is a true Gipsy proverb, used as a strongly marked indication of approbation or belief.

Kushto bak. Good luck!

As the Genoese of old greeted their friends with the word *Guadagna*! or "Gain!" indicating as Rabelais declares, their sordid character, so the Gipsy, whose life is precarious, and who depends upon chance for his daily bread, replies to "Sarishan!" (good day!) with "Kushto bak!" or "Good luck to you!" The Arabic "Baksheesh" is from the same root as bak, *i.e*., bacht.

When there's a boro bavol, *huller the tan parl the waver rikk pauli the bor*. When the wind is high, move the tent to the other side of the hedge behind it.

That is to say, change sides in an emergency.

"*Hatch apre! Hushti! The prastramengro's wellin! Jal the graias avree! Prastee*!"

"Jump up! Wide awake there! The policeman's coming! Run the horses off! Scamper!"

This is an alarm in camp, and constitutes a sufficiently graphic picture. The hint to run the horses off indicates a very doubtful title to their possession.

The prastramengro pens me mustn't hatch acai.

The policeman says we mustn't stop here.

No phrase is heard more frequently among Gipsies, who are continually in trouble with the police as to their right to stop and pitch their tents on commons.

I can hatch apre for pange (*panj*) *divvuses*.

I can stop here for five days.

A common phrase indicating content, and equivalent to, "I would like to sit here for a week."

The graias have taddered at the kas-stoggus -- we must jal an durer -- the gorgio's dicked us!

The horses have been pulling at the hay-stack--we must hurry away--the man has seen us!

When Gipsies have remained over night on a farm, it sometimes happens that their horses and asses--inadvertently of course--find their way to the haystacks or into a good field. *Humanum est errare*!

Yeck mush can lel a grai ta panni, *but twenty cant kair him pi*.

One man can take a horse to water, but twenty can't make him drink.

A well-known proverb.

A chirrico 'dree the mast is worth dui ' dree the bor.

A bird in the hand is worth two in the bush (hedge).

Never kin a pong dishler nor lel a romni by momeli dood.

Never buy a handkerchief nor choose a wife by candle-light.

Always jal by the divvus.

Always go by the day.

Chin tutes chuckko by tute's kaum.

Cut your coat according to your fancy. This is a Gipsy variation of an old proverb.

Fino ranyas kair fino trushnees.

Nice reeds make nice baskets.

He can't tool his kokerus togetherus (*kettenus*).

He can't hold himself together. Spoken of an infirm old man.

Too boot of a mush for his kokero.

Too much of a man for himself; *i.e*., he thinks too much of himself.

He's ***too boot of a mush to rakker a pauveri chavo***.

He's too proud too speak to a poor man. This was used, not in depreciation of a certain nobleman, whom the Gipsy who gave it to me had often seen, but admiringly, as if such ***hauteur*** were a commendable quality.

More (***koomi***) ***covvas the well***.

There are more things to come. Spoken of food on a table, and equivalent to "Don't go yet." ***The*** appears to be used in this as in many other instances, instead of ***to*** for the sake of euphony.

The jivaben has jawed avree out of his gad.

The life has gone out of his shirt, *i.e*., body. This intimates a long and close connection between the body and the under garment. "Avree out of," a phrase in which the Gipsy word is immediately followed by its English equivalent, is a common form of expression for the sake of clearness.

I toves my own gad.

I wash my own shirt.

A saying indicating celibacy or independence.

Mo rakkerfor a pennis when tute can't lel it.

Don't ask for a thing when you can't get it.

The wongurs kairs the grasni jal.

Money makes the mare go.

It's allers the boro matcho that pet-a-lay 'dree the panni.

It is always the largest fish that falls back into the water.

Bengis your see! ***Beng in tutes bukko***!

The devil in your heart. The devil in your body, or bowels.

This is a common form of imprecation among Gipsies all over the world.

Jawin sar a mush mullerin adree the boro naflo-ker.

Going like a man dying in the hospital.

Rikker it adree tute's kokero see an' kek'll jin.

Keep it a secret in your own heart, and nobody will know it.

Del sar mush a sigaben to hair his jivaben. Give every man a chance to make his living.

It's sim to a choomer, kushti for kek till it's pordered atween dui.

It's like a kiss, good for nothing until it is divided between two.

A cloudy sala often purabens to a fino divvus.

A cloudy morning often changes to a fine day.

Iuzhiou panni never jalled avree from a chickli tan.

Clean water never came out from a dirty place.

Sar mush must jal to the cangry, yeck divvus or the waver.

Every man must go to the church (*i.e*., be buried) some day or other.

Kek mush ever lelled adusta mongur.

No man ever got money enough.

Pale the wafri bak jals the kushti bak.

Behind bad luck comes good luck.

Saw mushis ain't got the sim kammoben as wavers.

All men have not the same tastes.

Lel the tacho pirro, an' it's pash kaired.

Well begun is half done.

Whilst tute's rakkerin the cheiruses jal.

While you are talking the *times* (hours) fly.

Wafri bak in a boro ker, *sim's adree a bitti her*.

There may be adversity in a large house as well as in a small one.

The kushtiest covvas allers jal avree siggest.

The best is soonest gone.

To dick a puro pal is as cammoben as a kushti habben.

To see an old friend is as agreeable as a good meal.

When tuti's pals chinger yeck with a waver, *don't tute jal adoi*.

When your brothers quarrel don't you meddle.

Pet up with the rakkerin an' mor pen chichi.

Endure the chattering and say nothing.

When a mush dels tute a grai tute man dick 'dree lester's mui.

When a man gives you a horse you must not look in his mouth.

Man jal atut the puvius.

Do not go across the field. Intimating that one should travel in the proper road.

There's a kushti sovaben at the kunsus of a duro drum.

There is a sweet sleep at the end of a long road.

Kair the cammodearer.

Make the best of it.

Rikker dovo adree tute's see.

Keep that a secret.

The koomi foki the tacho.

The more the merrier.

The pishom kairs the gudlo.

The bee makes the honey. *Id est*, each does his own work.

The pishom lels the gudlo avree the roozhers.

The bee gets honey from flowers. *Id est*, seeks it in the right place.

Hatch till the dood wells apre.

Wait till the moon rises. A very characteristic Gipsy saying.

Can't pen shukker atut lendy.

You cannot say aught against them.

He's boccalo ajaw to haw his chokkas.

He's hungry enough to eat his shoes.

The puro beng is a fino mush!

The devil is a nice character.

Mansha tu pal!

Cheer up, brother. Be a man! Spoken to any one who seems dejected. This corresponds partially to the German Gipsy *Manuschwari!* which is, however, rather an evil wish and a curse, meaning according to Dr Liebich (*Die Zigeuner*) the gallows, dire need, and epilepsy. Both in English and German it is, however, derived from Manusch, a man.

He's a hunnalo nakin mush.

He is an avaricious man. Literally, a spiteful nosed man.

Tute can hair a covva ferridearer if you jal shukar.

You can do a thing better if you go about it secretly.

We're lullero adoi we don't jin the jib.

We are dumb where we do not understand the language.

Chucked (chivved) saw the habben avree.

He threw all the victuals about. A melancholy proverb, meaning that state of irritable intoxication when a man comes home and abuses his family.

A myla that rikkers tute is kushtier to kistur than a grai that chivs you apre.

An ass that carries you is better than a horse that throws you off.

The juva, that sikkers her burk will sikker her bull.

"Free of her lips, free of her hips."

He sims mandy dree the mui -- like a puvengro.

He resembles me--like a potato.

Yeck hotchewitchi sims a waver as yeck bubby sims the waver.

One hedgehog is as like another as two peas.

He mored men dui.

He killed both of us. A sarcastic expression.

I dicked their stadees an langis sherros.

I saw their hats on their heads. Apropos of amazement at some very ordinary thing.

When you've tatti panni and rikker tutes kokero pash matto you can jal apre the wen sar a grai.

When you have brandy (spirits), and keep yourself half drunk, you can go through the winter like a horse.

CHAPTER VIII. INDICATIONS OF THE INDIAN ORIGIN OF THE GIPSIES.

Boro Duvel, or "Great God," an Old Gipsy term for Water--Bishnoo or Vishnu, the Rain-God--The Rain, called God's Blood by Gipsies--The Snow, "Angel's Feathers."--Mahadeva--Buddha--The Simurgh--The Pintni or Mermaid--The Nag or Blind-Worm--Nagari and Niggering--The Nile--Nats and Nautches, Naubat and Nobbet--A Puncher--Pitch, Piller and Pivlibeebee--Quod--Kishmet or Destiny--The Koran in England--"Sass"-- Sherengro--Sarserin--Shali or Rice--The Shaster in England--The Evil Eye--Sikhs--Stan, Hindostan, Iranistan--The true origin of Slang--Tat, the Essence of Being--Bahar and Bar--The Origin of the Words Rom and Romni.--Dom and Domni--The Hindi tem--Gipsy and Hindustani points of the Compass--Salaam and Shulam--Sarisham!--The Cups--Women's treading on objects--Horseflesh--English and Foreign Gipsies--Bohemian and Rommany.

A learned Sclavonian--Michael von Kogalnitschan--has said of Rommany, that he found it interesting to be able to study a Hindu dialect in the heart of Europe. He is quite right; but as mythology far surpasses any philology in interest, as regards its relations to poetry, how much more wonderful is it to find--to-day in England--traces of the tremendous avatars, whose souls were gods, long ago in India. And though these traces be faint, it is still apparent enough that they really exist.

One day an old Gipsy, who is said to be more than usually "deep" in Rommany, and to have had unusual opportunity for acquiring such knowledge from Gipsies older and deeper than himself, sent word to me, to know if "the rye" was aware that Boro Duvel, or the Great God, was an old Rommany expression for water? I thought that this was a singular message to come from a tent at Battersea, and asked my special Gipsy *factotum*, why God should be called water, or water, God? And he replied in the following words:

"Panni is the Boro Duvel, and it is Bishnoo or Vishnoo, because it pells alay from the Boro Duvel. '*Vishnu is the Boro Duvel then*?'--Avali. There can't be no stretch adoi--can there, rya? Duvel is Duvel all the world over--but by the right *formation*, Vishnoo is the Duvel's ratt. I've shuned adovo but dusta cheiruses. An' the snow is poris, that jals from the angels' winguses. And what I penned, that Bishnoo is the Duvel's ratt, is puro Rommanis, and jinned by saw our foki." {110}

Now in India, Vishnu and Indra are the gods of the rain.

The learned, who insist that as there ought to be, so there must be, but a single source of derivation for every word, ignoring the fact that a dozen causes may aid in its formation, will at once declare that, as Bishnoo or Vishnoo is derived from the old Gipsy Brishni or Brschindo, and this from the Hindu Barish, and the Sanscrit Varish or Prish, there can be "no rational ground" for connecting the English Gipsy word with the Hindu god. But who can tell what secret undercurrents of dim tradition and vague association may have come down to the present day from the olden time. That rain should be often called God's blood, and water bearing the name of Vishnu be termed God, and that this should be regarded as a specially curious bit of Gipsy lore, is at any rate remarkable enough.

As for the Gipsies in question ever having heard of Vishnu and other gods (as a friend suggests to me), save in this dim tradition, I can only say, that I doubt whether either of them ever heard even of the apostles; and I satisfied myself that the one who brought the secret had never heard of Joseph, was pitiably ignorant of Potiphar's wife, and only knew of "Mozhus" or Moses, that he "once heerd he was on the bulrushes."

Mahadeva, or Mahadev, exists apparently in the mouth of every English Gipsy in the phrase "Maduveleste!" or, God bless you. This word Maduvel is often changed to Mi--duvel, and is generally supposed to mean "My God;" but I was once assured, that the *old* and correct form was Ma, meaning great, and that it only meant great in connection with Duvel.

A curious illustration of a lost word returning by chance to its original source was given one day, when I asked a Gipsy if he knew such a word as Buddha? He promptly replied, "Yes; that a booderi or boodha mush was an *old* man;" and pointing to a Chinese image of Buddha, said: "That is a Boohda." He meant nothing more than that it represented an aged person, but the coincidence was at least remarkable. Budha in Hindustani really signifies an old man.

The same Gipsy, observing on the chimney-piece a quaint image of a Chinese griffin--a hideous little goblin with wings--informed me that the Gipsy name for it was a Seemor or Seemorus, and further declared that the same word meant a dolphin. "But a dolphin has no wings," I remarked. "Oh, hasn't it?" rejoined the Gipsy; "its *fins* are its wings, if it hadn't wings it could not be a Seemor." I think I recognise in this Seemor, the Simurgh or Griffin of Persian fable. {112} I could learn nothing more than this, that the Gipsy had always regarded a dolphin as resembling a large-headed winged monster, which he called a Seemor.

NAG is a snake in Hindustani. The English Gipsies still retain this primaeval word, but apply it only to the blind-worm. It is, however, remarkable that the Nag, or blind-worm, is, in the opinion of the Rommany, the most mysterious of creatures. I have been told that "when a nag mullers it's hardus as a kosh, and you can pogger it like a swagler's toov," "When a blind-worm dies it is as hard as a stick, and you can break it like a pipe-stem." They also believe that the Nag is gifted, so far as his will goes, with incredible malignity, and say of him--

    "If he could dick sim's he can shoon,   He wouldn't mukk mush or grai jal an the drum."

"If he could see as well as he can hear, he would not allow man or horse to go on the road."

The Hindi alphabet Deva Nagari, "the writing of the gods," is commonly called Nagari. A common English Gipsy word for writing is "niggering." "He niggered sar he could pooker adree a chinamangree." The resemblance between *nagari* and *nigger* may, it is true, be merely accidental, but the reader, who will ascertain by examination of the vocabulary the proportion of Rommany words unquestionably Indian, will admit that the terms have probably a common origin.

From Sanskrit to English Gipsy may be regarded as a descent "from the Nile to a street-gutter," but it is amusing at least to find a passable parallel for this simile. *Nill* in Gipsy is a rivulet, a river, or a gutter. Nala is in Hindustani a brook; nali, a kennel: and it has been conjectured that the Indian word indicates that of the great river of Egypt.

All of my readers have heard of the Nautch girls, the so-called *bayaderes* or dancing-girls of India; but very few, I suppose, are aware that their generic name is remotely preserved in several English Gipsy words. Nachna in Hindustani means to dance, while the Nats, who are a kind of Gipsies, are generally jugglers, dancers, and musicians. A *natua* is one of these Nats, and in English Gipsy *nautering* means going about with music. Other attractions may be added, but, as I have heard a Gipsy say, "it always takes music to go *a-nauterin'* or *nobbin'*."

Naubat in the language of the Hindu Nats signifies "time, turn, and instruments of music sounding at the gate of a great man, at certain intervals." "Nobbet," which is a Gipsy word well known to all itinerant negro minstrels, means to go about with music to get money. "To nobbet round the tem, bosherin'." It also implies time or turn, as I inferred from what I was told on inquiry. "You can shoon dovo at the wellgooras when yeck rakkers the waver, You jal and nobbet." "You can hear that at the fairs when one says to the other, You go and nobbet," meaning, "It is your turn to play now."

Nachna, to dance (Hindustani), appears to be reflected in the English Gipsy "nitchering," moving restlessly, fidgeting and dancing about. Nobbeting, I was told, "*is* nauterin'--it's all one, rya!"

Paejama in India means very loose trousers; and it is worth noting that Gipsies call loose leggings, trousers, or "overalls," peajamangris. This may be Anglo-Indian derived from the Gorgios. Whether "pea-jacket" belongs in part to this family, I will not attempt to decide.

Living constantly among the vulgar and uneducated, it is not to be wondered at that the English Gipsies should have often given a vulgar English and slangy term to many words originally Oriental. I have found that, without exception, there is a disposition among most people to promptly declare that all these words were taken, "of course," from English slang. Thus, when I heard a Gipsy speak of his fist as a "puncher," I naturally concluded that he did so because he regarded its natural use to be to "punch" heads with. But on asking him why he gave it that name, he promptly replied, "Because it takes pange (five) fingers to make a fist." And since *panja* means in Hindustani a hand with the five fingers extended, it is no violent assumption to conclude that even *puncher* may owe quite as much to Hindustani as to English, though I cheerfully admit that it would perhaps never have existed had it not been for English associations. Thus a Gipsy calls a pedlar a *packer* or *pack-mush*. Now, how much of this word is due to the English word pack or packer, and how much to *paikar*, meaning in Hindustani a pedlar? I believe that there has been as much of the one as of the other, and that this doubly-formative influence, or *influence of continuation*, should be seriously considered as regards all Rommany words which resemble in sound others of the same meaning, either in Hindustani or in English. It should also be observed that the Gipsy, while he is to the last degree inaccurate and a blunderer as regards *English* words (a fact pointed out long ago by the Rev. Mr Crabb), has, however, retained with great persistence hundreds of Hindu terms. Not being very familiar with peasant English, I have generally found Gipsies more intelligible in Rommany than in the language of their "stepfather-land," and have often asked my principal informant to tell me in Gipsy what I could not comprehend in "Anglo-Saxon."

"To pitch together" does not in English mean to stick together, although *pitch* sticks, but it does in Gipsy; and in Hindustani, *pichchi* means sticking or adhering. I find in all cases of such resemblance that the Gipsy word has invariably a closer affinity as regards meaning to the Hindu than to the English, and that its tendencies are always rather Oriental than Anglo-Saxon. As an illustration, I may point out *piller* (English Gipsy) to attack, having an affinity in *pilna* (Hindustani), with the same meaning. Many readers will at once revert to *pill*, *piller*, and *pillage*--all simply *implying* attack, but really meaning to *rob*, or robbery. But *piller* in English Gipsy also means, as in Hindustani, to assault indecently; and this is almost conclusive as to its Eastern origin.

It is remarkable that the Gipsies in England, or all the world over, have, like the Hindus, a distinctly descriptive expression for every degree of relationship. Thus a *pivli beebee* in English Gipsy, or *pupheri bahim* in Hindustani, is a father's sister's daughter. This in English, as in French or German, is simply a cousin.

Quod, imprisonment, is an old English cant and Gipsy word which Mr Hotten attempts to derive from a college quadrangle; but when we find that the Hindu *quaid* also means confinement, the probability is that it is to it we owe this singular term.

There are many words in which it is evident that the Hindu Gipsy meaning has been shifted from a cognate subject. Thus *putti*, the hub of a wheel in Gipsy, means the felly of a wheel in Hindustani. *Kaizy*, to rub a horse down, or scrape him, in the original tongue signifies "to tie up a horse's head by passing the bridle to his tail," to prevent his kicking while being rubbed or 'scraped. *Quasur*, or *kasur*, is in Hindustani flame: in English Gipsy *kessur* signifies smoke; but I have heard a Gipsy more than once apply the same term to flame and smoke, just as *miraben* stands for both life and death.

Very Oriental is the word kismet, or destiny, as most of my readers are probably aware. It is also English Gipsy, and was explained to me as follows: "A man's *kismut* is what he's bound to kair--it's the kismut of his see. Some men's kismut is better'n wavers, 'cos they've got more better chiv. Some men's kismut's to bikin grais, and some to bikin kanis; but saw foki has their kismut, an' they can't pen chichi elsus." In English, "A man's destiny is what he is bound to do--it is the fate of his soul (life). Some men's destiny is better than others, because they have more command of language. Some are fated to sell horses, and others to sell hens; but all people have their mission, and can do nothing else."

Quran in the East means the Koran, and quran uthara to take an oath. In English Gipsy kurran, or kurraben, is also an oath, and it seems strange that such a word from such a source should exist in England. It is, however, more interesting as indicating that the Gipsies did not leave India until familiarised with Mohammedan rule. "He kaired his kurran pre the Duvel's Bavol that he would jal 'vree the tem for a besh." "He swore his oath upon God's Breath (the Bible) that he would leave the country for a year." Upon inquiring of the Gipsy who uttered this phrase why he called the Bible "God's Breath," he replied naively, "It's sim to the Duvel's jivaben, just the same as His breathus." "It is like God's life, just the same as His breath."

It is to be observed that *nearly all the words which Gipsies claim as Gipsy, notwithstanding their resemblance to English, are to be found in Hindustani*. Thus *rutter*, to copulate, certainly resembles the English *rut*, but it is quite as much allied to *rutana* (Hindustani), meaning the same thing. "Sass," or sauce, meaning in Gipsy, bold, forward impudence, is identical with the same English word, but it agrees very well with the Hindu *sahas*, bold, and was perhaps born of the latter term, although it has been brought up by the former.

Dr A. F. Pott remarks of the German Gipsy word *schetra*, or violin, that he could nowhere find in Rommany a similar instrument with an Indian name. Sur-rhingee, or sarunghee, is the common Hindu word for a violin; and the English Gipsies, on being asked if they knew it, promptly replied that it was "an old word for the neck or head of a fiddle." It is true they also called it sarengro, surhingro, and shorengro, the latter word indicating that it might have been derived from sherro-engro-- *i.e.*, "head-thing." But after making proper allowance for the Gipsy tendency, or rather passion, for perverting words towards possible derivations, it seems very probable that the term is purely Hindu.

Zuhru, or Zohru, means in the East Venus, or the morning star; and it is pleas-ant to find a reflection of the rosy goddess in the Gipsy *soor*, signifying "early in the morning." I have been told that there is a Rommany word much resembling *soor*, meaning the early star, but my informant could not give me its exact sound. ***Dood of the sala*** is the common name for Venus. Sunrise is indicated by the eccentric term of "***kam-left the panni***" or sun-left the water. "It wells from the waver tem you jin," said my informant, in explanation. "The sun comes from a foreign coun-try, and first leaves that land, and then leaves the sea, before it gets here."

When a Gipsy is prowling for hens, or any other little waifs, and wishes to leave a broken trail, so that his tracks may not be identified, he will walk with the feet interlocked--one being placed outside the other--making what in America is very naturally termed a snake-trail. This he calls *sarserin*, and in Hindu *sarasana* means to creep along like a snake.

Supposing that the Hindu word for rice, *shali*, could hardly have been lost, I asked a Gipsy if he knew it, and he at once replied, "***Shali giv*** is small grain-corn, werry little grainuses indeed."

Shalita in Hindustani is a canvas sack in which a tent is carried. The English Gipsy has confused this word with *shelter*, and yet calls a small or "shelter" tent a shelter *gunno*, or bag. "For we rolls up the big tent in the shelter tent, to carry it." A tent cloth or canvas is in Gipsy a ***shummy***, evidently derived from the Hindu shumiyana, a canopy or awning.

It is a very curious fact that the English Gipsies call the Scripture or Bible the **Shaster**, and I record this with the more pleasure, since it fully establishes Mr Borrow as the first discoverer of the word in Rommany, and vindicates him from the suspicion with which his assertion was received by Dr Pott. On this subject the latter speaks as follows:--

"Eschastra de Moyses, l. ii. 22; [Greek text], M.; Sanskrit, castra; Hind., shastr, m. Hindu religious books, Hindu law, Scripture, institutes of science (Shakespeare). In proportion to the importance of the real existence of this word among the Gipsies must be the suspicion with which we regard it, when it depends, as in this instance, only on Borrow's assertion, who, in case of need, to supply a non-existing word, may have easily taken one from the Sanskrit."-- **Die Zigeuner**, vol. ii. p. 224.

The word **shaster** was given to me very distinctly by a Gipsy, who further volunteered the information, that it not only meant the Scriptures, but also any written book whatever, and somewhat marred the dignity of the sublime association of the Bible and Shaster, by adding that "any feller's bettin'-book on the race-ground was a **shasterni lil**, 'cos it's written."

I have never heard of the evil eye among the lower orders of English, but among Gipsies a belief in it is as common as among Hindus, and both indicate it by the same word, **seer** or **sihr**. In India **sihr**, it is true, is applied to enchantment or magic in general, but in this case the whole may very well stand for a part. I may add that my own communications on the subject of the **jettatura**, and the proper means of averting it by means of crab's claws, horns, and the usual sign of the fore and little finger, were received by a Gipsy auditor with great faith and interest.

To show, teach, or learn, is expressed in Gipsy by the word **sikker**, **sig**, or **seek**. The reader may not be aware that the Sikhs of India derive their name from the same root, as appears from the following extract from Dr Paspati's **etudes**: "**Sika-va**, v. prim. 1 cl. 1 conj. part, siklo', montrer, apprendre. Sanskrit, s'iks', to learn, to acquire science; siksaka, adj., a learner, a teacher. Hindustani, seek'hna, v.a., to learn, to acquire; seek'h, s.f., admonition." I next inquired why they were called Seeks, and they told me it was a word borrowed from one of the commandments of their founder, which signifies 'learn thou,' and that it was adopted to distinguish the sect soon after he disappeared. The word, as is well known, has the same import in the Hindoovee" ("Asiatic Researches," vol. i. p. 293, and vol. ii. p. 200). This was a noble word to give a name to a body of followers supposed to be devoted to knowledge and truth.

The English Gipsy calls a mermaid a ***pintni***; in Hindu it is ***bint ool buhr***, a maid of the sea. Bero in Gipsy is the sea or a ship, but the Rommany had reduced the term to the original ***bint***, by which a girl is known all over the East.

"Ya bint' Eeskendereyeh."

Stan is a word confounded by Gipsies with both ***stand***, a place at the races or a fair, and ***tan***, a stopping-place, from which it was probably derived. But it agrees in sound and meaning with the Eastern ***stan***, "a place, station," and by application "country," so familiar to the reader in Hindustan, Iranistan, Beloochistan, and many other names. It is curious to find in the Gipsy tan not only the root-word of a tent, but also the "Alabama," or "here we rest," applied by the world's early travellers to so many places in the Morning Land.

Slang does ***not*** mean, as Mr Hotten asserts, the secret language of the Gipsies, but is applied by them to acting; to speaking theatrical language, as in a play; to being an acrobat, or taking part in a show. It is a very old Gipsy word, and indicates plainly enough the origin of the cant word "slang." Using other men's words, and adopting a conventional language, strikes a Gipsy as ***artificial***; and many men not Gipsies express this feeling by speaking of conventional stage language as "theatrical slang." Its antiquity and origin appear in the Hindu swangi, an actor; swang, mockery, disguise, sham; and swang lena, to imitate. As regards the sound of the words, most English Gipsies would call swang "slang" as faithfully as a Cockney would exchange ***hat*** with '***at***.

Deepest among deep words in India is ***tat***, an element, a principle, the essence of being; but it is almost amusing to hear an English Gipsy say "that's the tatto (or tat) of it," meaning thereby "the thing itself," the whole of it. And thus the ultimate point of Brahma, and the infinite depth of all transcendental philosophy, may reappear in a cheap, portable, and convenient form, as a declaration that the real meaning of some mysterious transaction was that it amounted to a sixpenny swindle at thimble-rig; for to such base uses have the Shaster and the Vedas come in England.

It is, however, pleasant to find the Persian ***bahar***, a garden, recalling Bahar Danush, the garden of knowledge (Hindustani, bagh), reappearing in the English

Gipsy **bar**. "She pirryed adree the bar lellin ruzhers." "She walked in the garden plucking flowers." And it is also like old times and the Arabian Nights at home, to know that bazaar is a Gipsy word, though it be now quite obsolete, and signifies no longer a public street for shops, but an open field.

But of all words which identify the Gipsies with the East, and which prove their Hindu origin, those by which they call themselves Rom and Romni are most conclusive. In India the Dom caste is one of the lowest, whose business it is for the men to remove carcasses, while the Domni, or female Dom, sings at weddings. Everything known of the Dom identifies them with Gipsies. As for the sound of the word, any one need only ask the first Gipsy whom he meets to pronounce the Hindu *d* or the word Dom, and he will find it at once converted into *l* or *r*. There are, it is true, other castes and classes in India, such as Nats, the roving Banjaree, Thugs, &c., all of which have left unmistakable traces on the Gipsies, from which I conclude that at some time when these pariahs became too numerous and danger-ous there was a general expulsion of them from India. {124}

I would call particular attention to my suggestion that the Corn of India is the true parent of the Rom, because all that is known of the former caste indicates an affinity between them. The Dom pariahs of India who carry out or touch dead bod-ies, also eat the bodies of animals that have died a natural death, as do the Gipsies of England. The occupation of the Domni and Romni, dancing and making music at festivals, are strikingly allied. I was reminded of this at the last opera which I witnessed at Covent Garden, on seeing stage Gipsies introduced as part of the fete in "La Traviata."

A curious indication of the Indian origin of the Gipsies may be found in the fact that they speak of every foreign country beyond sea as the Hindi tem, Hindi being in Hindustani their own word for Indian. Nothing was more natural than that the Rommany on first coming to England should speak of far-away regions as being the same as the land they had left, and among such ignorant people the second genera-tion could hardly fail to extend the term and make it generic. At present an Irish-man is a **Hindi tem mush**, or Hindu; and it is rather curious, by the way, that a few years ago in America everything that was **anti**-Irish or native American received the same appellation, in allusion to the exclusive system of castes.

Although the Gipsies have sadly confounded the Hindu terms for the "cardinal points," no one can deny that their own are of Indian origin. Uttar is north in Hindustani, and Utar is west in Rommany. As it was explained to me, I was told that "Utar means west and wet too, because the west wind is wet." **Shimal** is also north in Hindu; and on asking a Gipsy what it meant, he promptly replied, "It's where the snow comes from." **Poorub** is the east in Hindustani; in Gipsy it is changed to porus, and means the west.

This confusion of terms is incidental to every rude race, and it must be constantly borne in mind that it is very common in Gipsy. Night suggests day, or black white, to the most cultivated mind; but the Gipsy confuses the name, and calls yesterday and to-morrow, or light and shadow, by the same word. More than this, he is prone to confuse almost all opposites on all occasions, and wonders that you do not promptly accept and understand what his own people comprehend. This is not the case among the Indians of North America, because oratory, involving the accurate use of words, is among them the one great art; nor are the negroes, despite their heedless ignorance, so deficient, since they are at least very fond of elegant expressions and forcible preaching. I am positive and confident that it would be ten times easier to learn a language from the wildest Indian on the North American continent than from any real English Gipsy, although the latter may be inclined with all his heart and soul to teach, even to the extent of passing his leisure days in "skirmishing" about among the tents picking up old Rommany words. Now the Gipsy has passed his entire life in the busiest scenes of civilisation, and is familiar with all its refined rascalities; yet notwithstanding this, I have found by experience that the most untutored Kaw or Chippewa, as ignorant of English as I was ignorant of his language, and with no means of intelligence between us save signs, was a genius as regards ability to teach language when compared to most Gipsies.

Everybody has heard of the Oriental **salaam**! In English Gipsy **shulam** means a greeting. "Shulam to your kokero!" is another form of **sarishan**! the common form of salutation. The Hindu **sar i sham** signifies "early in the evening," from which I infer that the Dom or Rom was a nocturnal character like the Night-Cavalier of Quevedo, and who sang when night fell, "Arouse ye, then, my merry men!" or who said "Good- evening!" just as we say (or used to say) "Good-day!" {127}

A very curious point of affinity between the Gipsies and Hindus may be found in a custom which was described to me by a Rom in the following words:--

"When a mush mullers, an' the juvas adree his ker can't *kair habben* because they feel so naflo 'bout the rom being gone, or the chavi or juvalo mush, or whoever it may be, then their friends for trin divvuses kairs their habben an' bitchers it a lende. An' that's tacho Rommanis, an' they wouldn't be dessen Rommany chuls that wouldn't kair dovo for mushis in sig an' tukli."

"When a man dies, and the women in his house cannot prepare food (literally, make food) as they feel so badly because the man is gone (or the girl, or young man, or whoever it may be), then their friends for three days prepare their food and send it to them. And that is real Rommany (custom), and they would not be decent Rommany fellows who would not do that for people in sorrow and distress."

Precisely the same custom prevails in India, where it is characterised by a phrase strikingly identical with the English Gipsy term for it. In England it is to *kair habben*, in Hindustani (Brice, Hin. Dict.) "karwa khana is the food that is sent for three days from relations to a family in which one of the members has died." The Hindu karwana, to make or to cause to do, and kara, to do, are the origin of the English Gipsy *kair* (to make or cook), while from khana, or 'hana, to eat, comes *haw* and *habben*, or food.

The reader who is familiar with the religious observances of India is probably aware of the extraordinary regard in which the cup is held by many sects. In Germany, as Mr Liebich declares, drinking-cups are kept by the Gipsies with superstitious regard, the utmost care being taken that they never fall to the ground. "Should this happen, the cup is *never* used again. By touching the ground it becomes sacred, and should no more be used. When a Gipsy cares for nothing else, he keeps his drinking-cup under every circumstance." I have not been able to ascertain whether this species of regard for the cup ever existed in England, but I know of many who could not be induced to drink from a white cup or bowl, the reason alleged being the very frivolous and insufficient one, that it reminded them of a blood-basin. It is almost needless to say that this could never have been the origin of the antipathy. No such consideration deters English peasants from using white crockery drinking-vessels.

In Germany, among the Gipsies, if a woman has trodden on any object, or if the skirt of her dress has swept over or touched it, it is either destroyed, or if of value, is disposed of or never used again. I found on inquiry that the same custom still prevails among the old Gipsy families in England, and that if the object be a crockery plate or cup, it is at once broken. For this reason, even more than for convenience, real Gipsies are accustomed to hang every cooking utensil, and all that pertains to the table, high up in their waggons. It is almost needless to point out how closely these ideas agree with those of many Hindus. The Gipsy eats every and any thing except horseflesh. Among themselves, while talking Rommany, they will boast of having eaten ***mullo baulors***, or pigs that have died a natural death, and ***hotche-witchi***, or hedgehog, as did the belle of a Gipsy party to me at Walton-on-Thames in the summer of 1872. They can give no reason whatever for this inconsistent abstinence. But Mr Simson in his "History of the Gipsies" has adduced a mass of curious facts, indicating a special superstitious regard for the horse among the Rommany in Scotland, and identifying it with certain customs in India. It would be a curious matter of research could we learn whether the missionaries of the Middle Ages, who made abstinence from horse-flesh a point of salvation (when preaching in Germany and in Scandinavia), derived their superstition, in common with the Gipsies, from India.

There can be no doubt that in seeking for the Indian origin of many Gipsy words we are often bewildered, and that no field in philology presents such opportunity for pugnacious critics to either attack or defend the validity of the proofs alleged. The very word for "doubtful" or "ambiguous," ***dubeni*** or ***dub'na***, is of this description. Is it derived from the Hindu ***dhoobd'ha***, which every Gipsy would pronounce ***doobna***, or from the English ***dubious***, which has been made to assume the Gipsy- Indian termination ***na***? Of this word I was naively told, "If a juva's bori (girl is big), that's ***dub'ni***; and if she's shuvalo (swelled up), ***that's*** dubni: for it may pen (say) she's kaired a tikno (is ***enceinte***), and it may pen she hasn't." But when we find that the English Gipsy also employs the word ***dukkeni*** for "doubtful," and compare it with the Hindustani ***dhokna*** or ***dukna***, the true derivation becomes apparent.

Had Dr Pott or Dr Paspati had recourse to the plan which I adopted of reading a copious Hindustani dictionary entirely through, word by word, to a patient Gipsy, noting down all which he recognised, and his renderings of them, it is very possible that these learned men would in Germany and Turkey have collected a mass of overwhelming proof as to the Indian origin of Rommany. At present the dictionary which I intend shall follow this work shows that, so far as the Rommany dialects have been published, that of England contains a far greater number of almost un-changed Hindu words than any other, a fact to which I would especially call the attention of all who are interested in this curious language. And what is more, I am certain that the supply is far from being exhausted, and that by patient research among old Gipsies, the Anglo-Rommany vocabulary might be increased to possibly five or six thousand words.

It is very possible that when they first came from the East to Europe the Gipsies had a very copious supply of words, for there were men among them of superior intelligence. But in Turkey, as in Germany, they have not been brought into such close contact with the ***Gorgios*** as in England: they have not preserved their famil-iarity with so many ideas, and consequently their vocabulary has diminished. Most of the Continental Gipsies are still wild, black wanderers, unfamiliar with many things for which the English Gipsy has at least a name, and to which he has contin-ued to apply old Indian words. Every one familiar with the subject knows that the English Gipsies in America are far more intelligent than their German Rommany cousins. A few years ago a large party of the latter appeared at an English race-course, where they excited much attention, but greatly disgusted the English Roms, not as rivals, but simply from their habits. "They couldn't do a thing but beg," said my informant. "They jinned (knew) nothing else: they were the dirtiest Gipsies I ever saw; and when the juvas suckled the children, they sikkered their burks (showed their breasts) as I never saw women do before foki." Such people would not, as a rule, know so many words as those who looked down on them.

The conclusion which I have drawn from studying Anglo-Rommany, and dif-ferent works on India, is that the Gipsies are the descendants of a vast number of Hindus, of the primitive tribes of Hindustan, who were expelled or emigrated from that country early in the fourteenth century. I believe they were chiefly of the primitive tribes, because evidence which I have given indicates that they were identical with the two castes of the Doms and Nats--the latter being, in fact, at the present day, the real Gipsies of India. Other low castes and outcasts were probably included in the emigration, but I believe that future research will prove that they were all of the old stock. The first Pariahs of India may have consisted entirely of those who refused to embrace the religion of their conquerors.

It has been coolly asserted by a recent writer that Gipsies are not proved to be of Hindu origin because "a few" Hindu words are to be found in their language. What the proportion of such words really is may be ascertained from the dictionary which will follow this work. But throwing aside all the evidence afforded by language, traditions, manners, and customs, one irrefutable proof still remains in the physical resemblance between Gipsies all the world over and the natives of India. Even in Egypt, the country claimed by the Gipsies themselves as their remote great-grandfather-land, the native Gipsy is not Egyptian in his appearance but Hindu. The peculiar brilliancy of the eye and its expression in the Indian is common to the Gipsy, but not to the Egyptian or Arab; and every donkey-boy in Cairo knows the difference between the **_Rhagarin_** and the native as to personal appearance. I have seen both Hindus in Cairo and Gipsies, and the resemblance to each other is as marked as their difference from Egyptians.

A few years ago an article on the Rommany language appeared in the "Atlantic Magazine" (Boston, U.S., America), in which the writer declared that Gipsy has very little affinity with Hindustani, but a great deal with Bohemian or Chech--in fact, he maintained, if I remember right, that a Chech and a Rom could understand one another in either of their respective tongues. I once devoted my time for several months to unintermitted study of Chech, and consequently do not speak in entire ignorance when I declare that true Rommany contains scores of Hindu words to one of Bohemian. {133}

CHAPTER IX. MISCELLANEA.

Gipsies and Cats.--"Christians."--Christians not "Hanimals."--Green, Red, and Yellow.--The Evil Eye.--Models and Morals.--Punji and Sponge-cake.--Troubles with a Gipsy Teacher.--Pilferin' and Bilberin'.--Khapana and Hopper.--Hoppera-glasses.--The little wooden Bear.--Huckeny Ponkee, Hanky Panky, Hocus-pocus, and Hokkeny Baro.--Burning a Gipsy Witch alive in America.--Daniel in the Lions' Den.--Gipsy Life in Summer.--The Gavengroes.--The Gipsy's Story of Pitch- and-Toss.--"You didn't fight your Stockings off?"--The guileless and venerable Gipsy.--The Gipsy Professor of Rommany and the Police.--His Delicacy of Feeling.--The old Gipsy and the beautiful Italian Models.--The Admired of the Police.--Honesty strangely illustrated.--Gipsies willing or unwilling to communicate Rommany.--Romance and Eccentricity of Gipsy Life and Manners.--The Gipsy Grandmother and her Family.--A fine Frolic interrupted.--The Gipsy Gentleman from America.--No such Language as Rommany.--Hedgehogs.--The Witch Element in Gipsy Life.--Jackdaws and Dogs.--Their Uses.--Lurchers and Poachers.--A Gipsy Camp.--The Ancient Henry.--I am mistaken for a Magistrate or Policeman.--Gipsies of Three Grades.--The Slangs.--Jim and the Twigs.--Beer rained from Heaven.--Fortune-telling.--A golden Opportunity to live at my Ease.--Petulamengro.--I hear of a New York Friend.--The Professor's Legend of the Olive-leaf and the Dove, "A wery tidy little Story."--The Story of Samson as given by a Gipsy.--The great Prize-fighter who was hocussed by a Fancy Girl.--The Judgment Day.--Passing away in Sleep or Dream to God.--A Gipsy on Ghosts.--Dogs which can kill Ghosts.--Twisted- legged Stealing.--How to keep Dogs away from a Place.--Gipsies avoid Unions.--A Gipsy Advertisement in the "Times."--A Gipsy Poetess and a Rommany Song.

It would be a difficult matter to decide whether the superstitions and odd fancies entertained by the Gipsies in England are derived from the English peasantry, were brought from India, or picked up on the way. This must be left for ethnologists more industrious and better informed than myself to decide. In any case, the possible common Aryan source will tend to obscure the truth, just as it often does the derivation of Rommany words. But nothing can detract from the inexpressibly quaint spirit of Gipsy originality in which these odd *credos* are expressed, or surpass the strangeness of the reasons given for them. If the spirit of the goblin and elfin lingers anywhere on earth, it is among the Rommany.

One day I questioned a Gipsy as to cats, and what his opinion was of black ones, correctly surmising that he would have some peculiar ideas on the subject, and he replied--

"Rommanys never lel kaulo matchers adree the ker, 'cause they're mullos, and beng is covvas; and the puro beng, you jin, is kaulo, an' has shtor herros an' dui mushis--an' a sherro. But pauno matchers san kushto, for they're sim to pauno ghosts of ranis."

Which means in English, "Gipsies never have black cats in the house, because they are unearthly creatures, and things of the devil; and the old devil, you know, is black, and has four legs and two arms--and a head. But white cats are good, for they are like the white ghosts of ladies."

It is in the extraordinary reason given for liking white cats that the subtle Gipsyism of this cat-commentary consists. Most people would consider a resemblance to a white ghost rather repulsive. But the Gipsy lives by night a strange life, and the reader who peruses carefully the stories which are given in this volume, will perceive in them a familiarity with goblin-land and its denizens which has become rare among "Christians."

But it may be that I do this droll old Gipsy great wrong in thus apparently classing him with the heathen, since he one day manifested clearly enough that he considered he had a right to be regarded as a true believer--the only drawback being this, that he was apparently under the conviction that all human beings were "Christians." And the way in which he declared it was as follows: I had given him the Hindustani word *janwur*, and asked him if he knew such a term, and he answered--

"Do I jin sitch a lav (know such a word) as *janwur* for a hanimal? Avo (yes); it's *jomper*--it's a toadus" (toad).

"But do you jin the lav (know the word) for an *animal*?"

"Didn't I just pooker tute (tell you) it was a jomper? for if a toad's a hanimal, *jomper* must be the lav for hanimal."

"But don't you jin kek lav (know a word) for sar the covvas that have jivaben (all living things)--for jompers, and bitti matchers (mice), and gryas (horses)? You and I are animals."

"Kek, rya, kek (no, sir, no), we aren't hanimals. *Hanimals* is critters that have something queer about 'em, such as the lions an' helephants at the well-gooroos (fairs), or cows with five legs, or won'ful piebald grais-- *them's* hanimals. But Christins aint hanimals. Them's *mushis*" (men).

To return to cats: it is remarkable that the colour which makes a cat desirable should render a bowl or cup objectionable to a true Gipsy, as I have elsewhere observed in commenting on the fact that no old-fashioned Rommany will drink, if possible, from white crockery. But they have peculiar fancies as to other colours. Till within a few years in Great Britain, as at the present day in Germany, their fondness for green coats amounted to a passion. In Germany a Gipsy who loses caste for any offence is forbidden for a certain time to wear green, so that *ver non semper viret* may be truly applied to those among them who bloom too rankly.

The great love for red and yellow among the Gipsies was long ago pointed out by a German writer as a proof of Indian origin, but the truth is, I believe, that all dark people instinctively choose these hues as agreeing with their complexion. A brunette is fond of amber, as a blonde is of light blue; and all true *kaulo* or dark Rommany *chals* delight in a bright yellow *pongdishler*, or neckerchief, and a red waistcoat. The long red cloak of the old Gipsy fortune-teller is, however, truly dear to her heart; she feels as if there were luck in it--that *bak* which is ever on Gipsy lips; for to the wanderers, whose home is the roads, and whose living is precarious, Luck becomes a real deity. I have known two old fortune-telling sisters to expend on new red cloaks a sum which seemed to a lady friend very considerable.

I have spoken in another chapter of the deeply-seated faith of the English Gipsies in the evil eye. Subsequent inquiry has convinced me that they believe it to be peculiar to themselves. One said in my presence, "There was a kauli juva that dicked the evil yack ad mandy the sala--my chavo's missis--an' a'ter dovo I shoo-ned that my chavo was naflo. A bongo-yacki mush kairs wafro-luckus. *Avali*, the Gorgios don't jin it--it's saw Rommany."

I.e., "There was a dark woman that looked the evil eye at me this morning--my son's wife--and after that I heard that my son was ill. A squint-eyed man makes bad-luck. Yes, the Gorgios don't know it--it's all Rommany."

The Gipsy is of an eminently social turn, always ready when occasion occurs to take part in every conversation, and advance his views. One day my old Rom hearing an artist speak of having rejected some uncalled- for advice relative to the employment of a certain model, burst out in a tone of hearty approbation with--

"That's what *I* say. Every man his own juva (every man his own girl), an' every painter his own *morals*."

If it was difficult in the beginning for me to accustom the Gipsy mind to reply clearly and consistently to questions as to his language, the trouble was tenfold increased when he began to see his way, as he thought, to my object, and to take a real interest in aiding me. For instance, I once asked--

"Puro! do you know such a word as *punji*? It's the Hindu for capital."

(Calmly.) "Yes, rya; that's a wery good word for capital."

"But is it Rommany?"

(Decidedly.) "It'll go first-rateus into Rommany."

"But can you make it out? Prove it!"

(Fiercely.) "Of course I can make it out. *Kushto*. Suppose a man sells 'punge-cake, would'nt that be his capital? *Punje* must be capital."

But this was nothing to what I endured after a vague fancy of the meaning of seeking a derivation of words had dimly dawned on his mind, and he vigorously attempted to aid me. Possessed with the crude idea that it was a success whenever two words could be forced into a resemblance of any kind, he constantly endea-voured to Anglicise Gipsy words--often, alas! an only too easy process, and could never understand why it was I then rejected them. By the former method I ran the risk of obtaining false Hindustani Gipsy words, though I very much doubt whether I was ever caught by it in a single instance; so strict were the tests which I adopted, the commonest being that of submitting the words to other Gipsies, or questioning him on them some days afterwards. By the latter "aid" I risked the loss of Rommany words altogether, and undoubtedly did lose a great many. Thus with the word ***bilber*** (to entice or allure), he would say, in illustration, that the girls ***bilbered*** the gentleman into the house to rob him, and then cast me into doubt by suggesting that the word must be all right, "'cause it looked all the same as ***pilferin'***."

One day I asked him if the Hindustani word khapana (pronounced almost hopana) (to make away with) sounded naturally to his ears.

"Yes, rya; that must be ***happer***, ***habber***, or ***huvver***. To hopper covvas away from the tan (***i.e***., to ***hopper*** things from the place), is when you rikker 'em awayus (carry them away, steal them), and gaverit (hide ***it***) tally your chuckko (under your coat). An' I can pen you a waver covva (I can tell you another thing) that's ***hopper***--them's the glasses that you look through-- ***hoppera***-glasses."

And here in bounding triumph he gave the little wooden bear a drink of ale, as if it had uttered this chunk of solid wisdom, and then treated himself to a good long pull. But the glance of triumph which shot from his black-basilisk eyes, and the joyous smile which followed these feats of philology, were absolutely irresistible. All that remained for me to do was to yield in silence.

One day we spoke of ***huckeny pokee***, or ***huckeny ponkee***, as it is sometimes called. It means in Rommany "sleight of hand," and also the adroit substitution of a bundle of lead or stones for another containing money or valuables, as practised by Gipsy women. The Gipsy woman goes to a house, and after telling the simple-minded and credulous housewife that there is a treasure buried in the cellar, persuades her that as "silver draws silver," she must deposit all her money or jewels in a bag near the place where the treasure lies. This is done, and the Rommany ***dye*** adroitly making up a parcel resembling the one laid down, steals the latter, leaving the former.

Mr Barrow calls this ***hokkeny baro***, the great swindle. I may remark, by the way, that among jugglers and "show-people" sleight of hand is called ***hanky panky***. "Hocus-pocus" is attributed by several writers to the Gipsies, a derivation which gains much force from the fact, which I have never before seen pointed out, that ***hoggu bazee***, which sounds very much like it, means in Hindustani legerdemain. English Gipsies have an extraordinary fancy for adding the termination ***us*** in a most irregular manner to words both Rommany and English. Thus *kettene* (together) is often changed to *kettenus*, and *side* to *sidus*. In like manner, *hog-gu* (*hocku* or *honku*) *bazee* could not fail to become *hocus bozus*, and the next change, for the sake of rhyme, would be to hocus-po- cus.

I told my ancient rambler of an extraordinary case of "huckeny pokee" which had recently occurred in the United States, somewhere in the west, the details of which had been narrated to me by a lady who lived at the time in the place where the event occurred.

"A Gipsy woman," I said, "came to a farmhouse and played huckeny pokee on a farmer's wife, and got away all the poor woman's money."

"Did she indeed, rya?" replied my good old friend, with a smile of joy flashing from his eyes, the unearthly Rommany light just glinting from their gloom.

"Yes," I said impressively, as a mother might tell an affecting story to a child. "All the money that that poor woman had, that wicked Gipsy woman took away, and utterly ruined her."

This was the culminating point; he burst into an irrepressible laugh; he couldn't help it--the thing had been done too well.

"But you haven't heard all yet," I added. "There's more covvas to well."

"Oh, I suppose the Rummany chi prastered avree (ran away), and got off with the swag?"

"No, she didn't."

"Then they caught her, and sent her to starabun" (prison).

"No," I replied.

"And what did they do?"

"THEY BURNT HER ALIVE!"

His jaw fell; a glossy film came over his panther-eyes. For a long time he had spoken to me, had this good and virtuous man, of going to America. Suddenly he broke out with this vehement answer--

"I won't go to that country-- *s'up mi duvel*! I'll never go to America."

It is told of a certain mother, that on showing her darling boy a picture in the Bible representing Daniel in the lions' den, she said, "And there is good Daniel, and there are those naughty lions, who are going to eat him all up." Whereupon the dear boy cried out, "O mother, look at that poor little lion in the corner--he won't get any."

It is from this point of view that such affairs are naturally regarded by the Rommany.

There is a strange goblinesque charm in Gipsydom--something of nature, and green leaves, and silent nights--but it is ever strangely commingled with the forbidden; and as among the Greeks of old with Mercury amid the singing of leafy brooks, there is a tinkling of, at least, petty larceny. Witness the following, which came forth one day from a Gipsy, in my presence, as an entirely voluntary utterance. He meant it for something like poetry--it certainly was suggested by nothing, and as fast as he spoke I wrote it down:--

"It's kushto in tattoben for the Rommany chals. Then they can jal langs the drum, and hatch their tan acai and odoi pre the tem. We'll lel moro habben acai, and jal andurer by-an'-byus, an' then jal by ratti, so's the Gorgios won't dick us. I jins a kushti puv for the graias; we'll hatch 'pre in the sala, before they latcher we've been odoi, an' jal an the drum an' lel moro habben."

"It is pleasant for the Gipsies in the summer-time. Then they can go along the road, and pitch their tent here and there in the land. We'll take our food here, and go further on by-and-by, and then go by night, so that the Gorgios won't see us. I know a fine field for the horses; we'll stop there in the morning, before they find we have been there, and go on the road and eat our food."

"I suppose that you often have had trouble with the *gavengroes* (police) when you wished to pitch your tent?"

Now it was characteristic of this Gipsy, as of many others, that when interested by a remark or a question, he would reply by bursting into some picture of travel, drawn from memory. So he answered by saying--

"They hunnelo'd the choro puro mush by pennin' him he mustn't hatch odoi. 'What's tute?' he pens to the prastramengro; 'I'll del you thrin bar to lel your chuckko offus an' koor mandy. You're a ratfully jucko an' a huckaben.'"

English --They angered the poor old man by telling him he must not stop there. "What are you?" he said to the policeman, "I'll give you three pounds to take your coat off and fight me. You're a bloody dog and a lie" (liar).

"I suppose you have often taken your coat off?"

"Once I lelled it avree an' never chivved it apre ajaw."

(*I.e.*, "Once I took it off and never put it on again.")

"How was that?"

"Yeckorus when I was a tano mush, thirty besh kenna--rummed about pange besh, but with kek chavis--I jalled to the prasters of the graias at Brighton. There was the paiass of wussin' the pasheros apre for wongur, an' I got to the pyass, an' first cheirus I lelled a boro bittus--twelve or thirteen bar. Then I nashered my wongur, an' penned I wouldn't pyass koomi, an' I'd latch what I had in my poachy. Adoi I jalled from the gudli 'dree the toss-ring for a pashora, when I dicked a waver mush, an' he putched mandy, 'What bak?' and I penned pauli, 'Kek bak; but I've got a bit-tus left.' So I wussered with lester an' nashered saw my covvas--my chukko, my gad, an' saw, barrin' my rokamyas. Then I jalled kerri with kek but my rokamyas an--I borried a chukko off my pen's chavo.

"And when my juva dickt'omandy pash-nango, she pens, 'Dovo's tute's heesis?' an' I pookered her I'd been a-koorin'. But she penned, 'Why, you haven't got your hovalos an; you didn't koor tute's hovalos avree?' 'No,' I rakkered; 'I taddered em offus. (The mush played me with a dui- sherro poshera.)

"But dree the sala, when the mush welled to lel avree the jucko (for I'd nash-ered dovo ajaw), I felt wafrodearer than when I'd nashered saw the waver covvas. An' my poor juva ruvved ajaw, for she had no chavo. I had in those divvuses as kushti coppas an' heesus as any young Gipsy in Anglaterra--good chukkos, an' gads, an' pongdishlers.

"An' that mush kurried many a geero a'ter mandy, but he never lelled no bak. He'd chore from his own dadas; but he mullered wafro adree East Kent."

"Once when I was a young man, thirty years ago (now)--married about five years, but with no children--I went to the races at Brighton. There was tossing halfpence for money, and I took part in the game, and at first (first time) I took a good bit--twelve or thirteen pounds. Then I lost my money, and said I would play no more, and would keep what I had in my pocket. Then I went from the noise in the toss-ring for half an hour, when I saw another man, and he asked me, 'What luck?' and I replied, 'No luck; but I've a little left yet.' So I tossed with him and lost all my things--my coat, my shirt, and all, except my breeches. Then I went home with nothing but my breeches on--I borrowed a coat of my sister's boy.

"And when my wife saw me half-naked, she *says*, 'Where are your clothes?'

and I told her I had been fighting. But she said, 'Why, you have not your stockings on; you didn't fight your stockings off!' 'No,' I said; 'I drew them off.' (The man played me with a two-headed halfpenny.)

"But in the morning when the man came to take away the dog (for I had lost that too), I felt worse than when I lost all the other things. And my poor wife cried again, for she had no child. I had in those days as fine clothes as any young Gipsy in England--good coats, and shirts, and handkerchiefs.

"And that man hurt many a man after me, but he never had any luck. He'd steal from his own father; but he died miserably in East Kent."

It was characteristic of the venerable wanderer who had installed himself as my permanent professor of Rommany, that although almost every phrase which he employed to illustrate words expressed some act at variance with law or the rights of property, he was never weary of descanting on the spotlessness, beauty, and integrity of his own life and character. These little essays on his moral perfection were expressed with a touching artlessness and child-like simplicity which would carry conviction to any one whose heart had not been utterly hardened, or whose eye-teeth had not been remarkably well cut, by contact with the world. In his delightful ***naivete*** and simple earnestness, in his ready confidence in strangers and freedom from all suspicion--in fact, in his whole deportment, this Rommany elder reminded me continually of one--and of one man only--whom I had known of old in America. Need I say that I refer to the excellent --- ---?

It happened for many days that the professor, being a man of early habits, arrived at our rendezvous an hour in advance of the time appointed. As he resolutely resisted all invitation to occupy the room alone until my arrival, declaring that he had never been guilty of such a breach of etiquette, and as he was, moreover, according to his word, the most courteous man of the world in it, and I did not wish to "contrary" him, he was obliged to pass the time in the street, which he did by planting himself on the front steps or expanding himself on the railings of an elderly and lonely dame, who could not endure that even a mechanic should linger at her door, and was in agony until the milkman and baker had removed their feet from her steps. Now, the appearance of the professor (who always affected the old Gipsy style), in striped corduroy coat, leather breeches and gaiters, red waistcoat, yellow neck-handkerchief, and a frightfully-dilapidated old white hat, was not, it must be admitted, entirely adapted to the exterior of a highly respectable mansion. "And he had such a vile way of looking, as if he were a-waitin' for some friend to come out o' the 'ouse." It is almost needless to say that this apparition attracted the police from afar off and all about, or that they gathered around him like buzzards near a departed lamb. I was told by a highly intelligent gentleman who witnessed the interviews, that the professor's kindly reception of these public characters--the infantile smile with which he courted their acquaintance, and the good old grand-fatherly air with which he listened to their little tales--was indescribably delight-ful. "In a quarter of an hour any one of them would have lent him a shilling;" and it was soon apparent that the entire force found a charm in his society. The lone lady herself made a sortie against him once; but one glance at the amiable smile, "which was child-like and bland," disarmed her, and it was reported that she subsequently sent him out half-a-pint of beer.

It is needless to point out to the reader accustomed to good society that the professor's declining to sit in a room where valuable and small objects abounded, in the absence of the owner, was dictated by the most delicate feeling. Not less remarkable than his strict politeness was the mysterious charm which this antique nomad unquestionably exercised on the entire female sex. Ladies of the highest re-spectability and culture, old or young, who had once seen him, invariably referred to him as "that charming old Gipsy."

Nor was his sorcery less potent on those of low degree. Never shall I forget one morning when the two prettiest young Italian model-girls in all London were poseeing to an artist friend while the professor sat and imparted to me the lore of the Rommany. The girls behaved like moral statues till he appeared, and like quicksilver imps and devilettes for the rest of the sitting. Something of the wild and weird in the mountain Italian life of these ex-contadine seemed to wake like unholy fire, and answer sympathetically to the Gipsy wizard-spell. Over mountain and sea, and through dark forests with legends of *streghe* and Zingari, these semi-outlaws of society, the Neapolitan and Rommany, recognised each other intuitively. The handsomest young gentleman in England could not have interested these hand-some young sinners as the dark-brown, grey-haired old vagabond did. Their eyes stole to him. Heaven knows what they talked, for the girls knew no English, but they whispered; they could not write little notes, so they kept passing different objects, to which Gipsy and Italian promptly attached a meaning. Scolding them helped not. It was "a pensive sight."

To impress me with a due sense of his honesty and high character, the professor informed me one day that he was personally acquainted, as he verily believed, with every policeman in England. "You see, rya," he remarked, "any man as is so well known couldn't never do nothing wrong now,--could he?"

Innocent, unconscious, guileless air--and smile! I shall never see its equal. I replied--

"Yes; I think I can see you, Puro, walking down between two lines of hundreds of policemen--every one pointing after you and saying, 'There goes that good honest --- the honestest man in England!'"

"Avo, rya," he cried, eagerly turning to me, as if delighted and astonished that I had found out the truth. "That's just what they all pens of me, an' just what I seen 'em a-doin' every time."

"You know all the police," I remarked. "Do you know any turnkeys?"

He reflected an instant, and then replied, artlessly--

"I don't jin many o' them. But I can jist tell you a story. Once at Wimbledown, when the *kooroo-mengroes* were *odoi* (when the troopers were there), I used to get a pound a week carryin' things. One day, when I had well on to two stun on my *dumo* (back), the chief of police sees me an' says, 'There's that old scoundrel again! that villain gives the police more trouble than any other man in the country!' 'Thank you, sir,' says I, wery respectable to him. 'I'm glad to see you're earnin' a 'onest livin' for once,' says he. 'How much do you get for carryin' that there bundle?' 'A sixpence, rya!' says I. 'It's twice as much as you ought to have,' says he; 'an' I'd be glad to carry it myself for the money.' 'All right, sir,' says I, touchin' my hat and goin' off, for he was a wery nice gentleman. Rya," he exclaimed, with an air of placid triumph, "do you think the head-police his selfus would a spoke in them wery words to me if he hadn't a thought I was a good man?"

"Well, let's get to work, old Honesty. What is the Rommanis for to hide?"

"To *gaverit* is to hide anything, rya. *Gaverit*." And to illustrate its application he continued--

"They penned mandy to gaver the gry, but I nashered to keravit, an' the mush who lelled the gry welled alangus an' dicked it."

("They told me to hide the horse, but I forgot to do it, and the man who **owned** the horse came by and saw it.")

It is only a few hours since I heard of a gentleman who took incredible pains to induce the Gipsies to teach him their language, but never succeeded. I must confess that I do not understand this. When I have met strange Gipsies, it has often greatly grieved me to find that they spoke their ancient tongue very imperfectly, and were ignorant of certain Rommany words which I myself, albeit a stranger, knew very well, and would fain teach them. But instead of accepting my instructions in a docile spirit of ignorant humility, I have invariably found that they were eagerly anxious to prove that they were not so ignorant as I assumed, and in vindication of their intelligence proceeded to pour forth dozens of words, of which I must admit many were really new to me, and which I did not fail to remember.

The scouting, slippery night-life of the Gipsy; his familiarity with deep ravine and lonely wood-path, moonlight and field-lairs; his use of a secret language, and his constant habit of concealing everything from everybody; his private superstitions, and his inordinate love of humbugging and selling friend and foe, tend to produce in him that goblin, elfin, boyish-mischievous, out-of-the-age state of mind which is utterly indescribable to a prosaic modern-souled man, but which is delightfully piquant to others. Many a time among Gipsies I have felt, I confess with pleasure, all the subtlest spirit of fun combined with picture-memories of Hayraddin Maugrabin--witch-legends and the "Egyptians;" for in their ignorance they are still an unconscious race, and do not know what the world writes about them. They are not attractive from the outside to those who have no love for quaint scholarship, odd humours, and rare fancies. A lady who had been in a camp had nothing to say of them to me save that they were "dirty--dirty, and begged." But I ever think, when I see them, of Tieck's Elves, and of the Strange Valley, which was so grim and repulsive from without, but which, once entered, was the gay forecourt of goblin-land.

The very fact that they hide as much as they can of their Gipsy life and nature from the Gorgios would of itself indicate the depths of singularity concealed beneath their apparent life--and this reminds me of incidents in a Sunday which I once passed beneath a Gipsy roof. I was, **en voyage**, at a little cathedral town, when learning that some Gipsies lived in a village eight miles distant, I hired a carriage and rode over to see them. I found my way to a neat cottage, and on entering it discovered that I was truly enough among the Rommany. By the fire sat a well-dressed young man; near him was a handsome, very dark young woman, and there presently entered a very old woman,--all gifted with the unmistakable and peculiar expression of real Gipsies.

The old woman overwhelmed me with compliments and greetings. She is a local celebrity, and is constantly visited by the most respectable ladies and gentlemen. This much I had learned from my coachman. But I kept a steady silence, and sat as serious as Odin when he visited the Vala, until the address ceased. Then I said in Rommany--

"Mother, you don't know me. I did not come here to listen to fortune- telling."

To which came the prompt reply, "I don't know what the gentleman is saying." I answered always in Rommany.

"You know well enough what I am saying. You needn't be afraid of me--I'm the nicest gentleman you ever saw in all your life, and I can talk Rommany as fast as ever you ran away from a policeman."

"What language is the gentleman talking?" cried the old dame, but laughing heartily as she spoke.

"Oh dye--miri dye, Don't tute jin a Rommany rye? Can't tu rakker Rommany jib, Tachipen and kek fib?"

"Avo, my rye; I can understand you well enough, but I never saw a Gipsy gentleman before."

[Since I wrote that last line I went out for a walk, and on the other side of Walton Bridge, which legend says marks the spot where Julius Caesar crossed, I saw a tent and a waggon by the hedge, and knew by the curling blue smoke that a Gipsy was near. So I went over the bridge, and sure enough there on the ground lay a full-grown Petulamengro, while his brown *juva* tended the pot. And when I spoke to her in Rommany she could only burst out into amazed laughter as each new sentence struck her ear, and exclaim, "Well! well! that ever I should live to hear this! Why, the gentleman talks just like one of *us*! '*Bien apropos*,' sayde ye ladye."]

"Dye," quoth I to the old Gipsy dame, "don't be afraid. I'm *tacho*. And shut that door if there are any Gorgios about, for I don't want them to hear our *rak-*

kerben. Let us take a drop of brandy--life is short, and here's my bottle. I'm not English--I'm a **waver temmeny mush** (a foreigner). But I'm all right, and you can leave your spoons out. Tacho."

> "The boshno an' kani
> The rye an' the rani;
> Welled acai 'pre the boro lun pani.
> Rinkeni juva hav acai!
> Del a choomer to the rye!"

"**Duveleste**!" said the old fortune-teller, "that ever I should live to see a rye like you! A boro rye rakkerin' Rommanis! But you must have some tea now, my son--good tea."

"I don't pi muttermengri dye ('drink tea,' but an equivoque). It's muttermengri with you and with us of the German jib."

"Ha! ha! but you must have food. You won't go away like a Gorgio without tasting anything?"

"I'll eat bread with you, but tea I haven't tasted this five-and-twenty years."

"Bread you shall have, rya." And saying this, the daughter spread out a clean white napkin, and placed on it excellent bread and butter, with plate and knife. I never tasted better, even in Philadelphia. Everything in the cottage was scrupulously neat--there was even an approach to style. The furniture and ornaments were superior to those found in common peasant houses. There was a large and beautifully-bound photograph album. I found that the family could read and write--the daughter received and read a note, and one of the sons knew who and what Mr Robert Browning was.

But behind it all, when the inner life came out, was the wild Rommany and the witch-*aura*--the fierce spirit of social exile from the world in which they lived (the true secret of all the witch-life of old), and the joyous consciousness of a secret tongue and hidden ways. To those who walk in the darkness of the dream, let them go as deep and as windingly as they will, and into the grimmest gloom of goblin-land, there will never be wanting flashes of light, though they be gleams diavoline, corpse-candlelights, elfin sparkles, and the unearthly blue lume of the eyes of silent night-hags wandering slow. In the forgotten grave of the sorcerer burns steadily through long centuries the Rosicrucian lamp, and even to him whose eyes are closed, sparkle, on pressure, phosphorescent rings. So there was Gipsy laughter; and the ancient *wicca* and Vala flashed out into that sky-rocketty joyousness and Catherine-wheel gaiety, which at eighty or ninety, in a woman, vividly reminds one of the Sabbat on the Brocken, of the ointment, and all things terrible and un-earthly and forbidden.

I do not suppose that there are many people who can feel or understand that among the fearfully dirty dwellers in tents and caravans, cock-shysters and deal-ers in dogs of doubtful character, there can be anything strange, and quaint, and deeply tinged with the spirit of which I have spoken. As well might one attempt to persuade the twenty-stone half-illiterate and wholly old-fashioned rural magistrate of the last century that the poor devil of a hen-stealing Gipsy dragged before him knew that which would send thrills of joy through the most learned philologist in Europe, and cause the great band of scholars to sing for joy. Life, to most of us, is nothing without its humour; and to me a whilome German student illustrating his military marauding by phrases from Fichte, or my friend Pauno the Rommany urg-ing me with words to be found in the Mahabahrata and Hafiz to buy a terrier, is a charming experience.

I believe that my imagination has neither been led nor driven, when it has so invariably, in my conversing with Gipsy women, recalled Faust, and all I have ever read in Wierus, Bodinus, Bekker, Mather, or Glanvil, of the sorceress and *sortilega*. And certainly on this earth I never met with such a perfect *replica* of Old Mother Baubo, the mother of all the witches, as I once encountered at a certain race. Swar-thy, black-eyed, stout, half-centuried, fiercely cunning, and immoderately sensual, her first salutation was expressed in a phrase such as a Corinthian soul might be greeted with on entering that portion of the after-world devoted to the fastest of the fair. With her came a tall, lithe, younger sorceress; and verily the giant fat sow for her majesty, and the broom for the attendant, were all that was wanting.

To return to the cottage. Our mirth and fun grew fast and furious; the family were delighted with my anecdotes of the Rommany in other lands--German, Bohe-mian, and Spanish,--not to mention the *gili*. And we were just in the gayest centre of it all, "whin,--och, what a pity!--this fine tay-party was suddenly broken up," as

Patrick O'Flanegan remarked when he was dancing with the chairs to the devil's fiddling, and his wife entered. For in rushed a Gipsy boy announcing that Gorgios (or, as I may say, "wite trash") were near at hand, and evidently bent on entering. That this irruption of the enemy gave a taci-turn to our riotry and revelling will be believed. I tossed the brandy in the cup into the fire; it flashed up, and with it a quick memory of the spilt and blazing witch-brew in "Faust." I put the tourist-flask in my pocket, and in a trice had changed my seat and assumed the air of a chance intruder. In they came, two ladies--one decidedly pretty--and three gentlemen, all of the higher class, as they indicated by their manner and language. They were almost immediately followed by a Gipsy, the son of my hostess, who had sent for him that he might see me.

He was a man of thirty, firmly set, and had a stern hard countenance, in which shone two glittering black eyes, which were serpent-like even among the Rommany. Nor have I ever seen among his people a face so expressive of self-control allied to wary suspicion. He was neatly dressed, but in a subdued Gipsy style, the principal indication being that of a pair of "cords," which, however, any gentleman might have worn--in the field. His English was excellent--in fact, that of an educated man; his sum total that of a very decided "character," and one who, if you wronged him, might be a dangerous one.

We entered into conversation, and the Rommany rollicking seemed all at once a vapoury thing of the dim past; it was the scene in a witch-revel suddenly shifted to a drawing-room in May Fair. We were all, and all at once, so polite and gentle, and so readily acquainted and cosmo-polite--quite beyond the average English standard; and not the least charming part of the whole performance was the skill with which the minor parts were filled up by the Gipsies, who with exquisite tact followed our lead, seeming to be at once hosts and guests. I have been at many a play, but never saw anything better acted.

But under it all burnt a lurid though hidden flame; and there was a delightful *diablerie* of concealment kept up among the Rommany, which was the more exquisite because I shared in it. Reader, do you remember the scene in George Borrow's "Gipsies in Spain," in which the woman blesses the child in Spanish, and mutters curses on it meanwhile in Zincali? So it was that my dear old hostess blessed the sweet young lady, and "prodigalled" compliments on her; but there was one instant when her eye met mine, and a soft, quick-whispered, wicked Rommany phrase, unheard by the ladies, came to my ear, and in the glance and word there was a concentrated anathema.

The stern-eyed Gipsy conversed well, entertaining his guests with ease. After he had spoken of the excellent behaviour and morals of his tribe--and I believe that they have a very high character in these respects--I put him a question.

"Can you tell me if there is really such a thing as a Gipsy language? one hears such differing accounts, you know."

With the amiable smile of one who pitied my credulity, but who was himself superior to all petty deception or vulgar mystery, he replied--

"That is another of the absurd tales which people have invented about Gipsies. As if we could have kept such a thing a secret!"

"It does, indeed, seem to me," I replied, "that if you *had*, some people who were not Gipsies *must* have learned it."

"Of course," resumed the Gipsy, philosophically, "all people who keep together get to using a few peculiar terms. Tailors and shoemakers have their own words. And there are common vagabonds who go up and down talking thieves' slang, and imposing it on people for Gipsy. But as for any Gipsy tongue, I ought to know it" ("So I should think," I mentally ejaculated, as I contemplated his brazen calmness); "and I don't know three words of it."

And we, the Gorgios, all smiled approval. At least that humbug was settled; and the Rommany tongue was done for--dead and buried--if, indeed, it ever existed. Indeed, as I looked in the Gipsy's face, I began to realise that a man might be talked out of a belief in his own name, and felt a rudimentary sensation to the effect that the language of the Black Wanderers was all a dream, and Pott's Zigeuner the mere tinkling of a pot of brass, Paspati a jingling Turkish symbol, and all Rommany a ***praeterea nihil*** without the ***vox***. To dissipate the delusion, I inquired of the Gipsy--

"You have been in America. Did you ever hunt game in the west?"

"Yes; many a time. On the plains."

"Of course--buffalo--antelope--jack rabbits. And once" (I said this as if forgetfully)--"I once ate a hedgehog--no, I don't mean a hedgehog, but a porcupine."

A meaning glance shot from the Gipsy's eye. I uttered a first-class password, and if he had any doubt before as to who the Rommany rye might be, there was none now. But with a courteous smile he replied--

"It's quite the same, sir--porcupine or hedgehog. I know perfectly well what you mean."

"Porcupines," I resumed, "are very common in America. The Chippeways call them *hotchewitchi*."

This Rommany word was a plumper for the Gipsy, and the twinkle of his eye--the smallest star of mirth in the darkest night of gravity I ever beheld in my life--was lovely. I had trumped his card at any rate with as solemn gravity as his own; and the Gorgios thought our reminiscences of America were very entertaining.

"He had more tow upon his distaffe   Than Gervais wot of."

But there was one in the party--and I think only one--who had her own private share in the play. That one was the pretty young lady. Through all the conversation, I observed from time to time her eyes fixed on my face, as if surmising some unaccountable mystery. I understood it at once. The bread and butter on the table, partly eaten, and the snow-white napkin indicated to a feminine eye that some one not of the household had been entertained, and that I was the guest. Perhaps she had seen the old woman's quick glance at me, but it was evident that she felt a secret. What she divined I do not know. Should this work ever fall into her hands, she will learn it all, and with it the fact that Gipsies can talk double about as well as any human beings on the face of the earth, and enjoy fun with as grave a face as any Ojib'wa of them all.

The habits of the Gipsy are pleasantly illustrated by the fact that the collection of "animated books," which no Rommany gentleman's library should be without, generally includes a jackdaw. When the foot of the Gorgio is heard near the tent, a loud "*wa-awk*" from the wary bird (sounding very much like an alarm) at once proclaims the fact; and on approaching, the stranger finds the entire party in all probability asleep. Sometimes a dog acts as sentinel, but it comes to the same thing. It is said you cannot catch a weasel asleep: I am tempted to add that you can never find a Gipsy awake--but it means precisely the same thing.

Gipsies are very much attached to their dogs, and in return the dogs are very much attached to their masters--so much so that there are numerous instances, perfectly authenticated, of the faithful animals having been in the habit of ranging the country alone, at great distances from the tent, and obtaining hares, rabbits, or other game, which they carefully and secretly brought by night to their owners as a slight testimonial of their regard and gratitude. As the dogs have no moral appreciation of the Game Laws, save as manifested in gamekeepers, no one can blame them. Gipsies almost invariably prefer, as canine manifesters of devotion, lurchers, a kind of dog which of all others can be most easily taught to steal. It is not long since a friend of mine, early one morning between dark and dawn, saw a lurcher crossing the Thames with a rabbit in his mouth. Landing very quietly, the dog went to a Gipsy *tan*, deposited his burden, and at once returned over the river.

Dogs once trained to such secret hunting become passionately fond of it, and pursue it unweariedly with incredible secrecy and sagacity. Even cats learn it, and I have heard of one which is "good for three rabbits a week." Dogs, however, bring everything home, while puss feeds herself luxuriously before thinking of her owner. But whether dog or cat, cock or jackdaw, all animals bred among Gipsies do unquestionably become themselves Rommanised, and grow sharp, and shrewd, and mysterious. A writer in the ***Daily News*** of October 19, 1872, speaks of having seen parrots which spoke Rommany among the Gipsies of Epping Forest. A Gipsy dog is, if we study him, a true character. Approach a camp: a black hound, with sleepy eyes, lies by a tent; he does not bark at you or act uncivilly, for that forms no part of his master's life or plans, but wherever you go those eyes are fixed on you. By-and-by he disappears--he is sure to do so if there are no people about the *tan*--and then reappears with some dark descendant of the Dom and Domni. I have always been under the impression that these dogs step out and mutter a few words in Rommany--their deportment is, at any rate, Rommanesque to the highest degree, indicating a transition from the barbarous silence of doghood to Christianly intelligence. You may persuade yourself that the Gipsies do not mind your presence, but rest assured that though he may lie on his side with his back turned, the cunning *jucko* is carefully noting all you do. The abject and humble behaviour of a poor negro's dog in America was once proverbial: the quaint shrewdness, the droll roguery, the demure devilry of a real Gipsy dog are beyond all praise.

The most valuable dogs to the Gipsies are by no means remarkable for size or beauty, or any of the properties which strike the eye; on the contrary, an ugly, shirking, humble-looking, two-and-sixpenny-countenanced cur, if he have but in-tellect, is much more their *affaire*. Yesterday morning, while sitting among the tents of "ye Egypcians," I overheard a knot of men discussing the merits of a degrad-ed-looking doglet, who seemed as if he must have committed suicide, were he only gifted with sense enough to know how idiotic he looked. "Would you take seven pounds for him?" asked one. "Avo, I would take seven bar; but I wouldn't take six, nor six an' a half neither."

The stranger who casts an inquisitive eye, though from afar off, into a Gipsy camp, is at once noted; and if he can do this before the wolf--I mean the Rom--sees him, he must possess the gift of fern-seed and walk invisible, as was illustrated by the above-mentioned yesterday visit. Passing over the bridge, I paused to admire the scene. It was a fresh sunny morning in October, the autumnal tints were beau-tiful in golden brown or oak red, while here and there the horse-chestnuts spread their saffron robes, waving in the embraces of the breeze like hetairae of the for-est. Below me ran the silver Thames, and above a few silver clouds--the belles of the air--were following its course, as if to watch themselves in the watery winding mirror. And near the reedy island, at the shadowy point always haunted by three swans, whom I suspect of having been there ever since the days of Odin-faith, was the usual punt, with its elderly gentlemanly gudgeon-fishers. But far below me, along the dark line of the hedge, was a sight which completed the English character of the scene--a real Gipsy camp. Caravans, tents, waggons, asses, smouldering fires; while among them the small forms of dark children could be seen frolicking about. One Gipsy youth was fishing in the stream from the bank, and beyond him a knot of busy basketmakers were visible.

I turned the bridge, adown the bank, and found myself near two young men mending chairs. They greeted me civilly; and when I spoke Rommany, they an-swered me in the same language; but they did not speak it well, nor did they, in-deed, claim to be "Gipsies" at all, though their complexions had the peculiar hue which indicates some other than Saxon admixture of blood. Half Rommany in their knowledge, and yet not regarded as such, these "travellers" represented a very large class in England, which is as yet but little understood by our writers, whether of fact or fiction. They laughed while telling me anecdotes of gentlemen who had mistaken them for real Rommany chals, and finally referred me to "Old Henry," further down, who "could talk with me." This ancient I found a hundred yards beyond, basketing in the sun at the door of his tent. He greeted me civilly enough, but worked away with his osiers most industriously, while his comrades, less busy, employed themselves vigorously in looking virtuous. One nursed his infant with tender embraces, another began to examine green sticks with a view to converting them into clothes-pegs--in fact I was in a model community of wandering Shakers.

I regret to say that the instant I uttered a Rommany word, and was recognised, this discipline of decorum was immediately relaxed. It was not complimentary to my moral character, but it at least showed confidence. The Ancient Henry, who bore, as I found, in several respects a strong likeness to the Old Harry, had heard of me, and after a short conversation confided the little fact, that from the moment in which I had been seen watching them, they were sure I was a *gav-mush*, or police or village authority, come to spy into their ways, and to at least order them to move on. But when they found that I was not as one having authority, but, on the contrary, came talking Rommany with the firm intention of imparting to them three pots of beer just at the thirstiest hour of a warm day, a great change came over their faces. A chair was brought to me from a caravan at some distance, and I was told the latest news of the road.

"Matty's got his slangs," observed Henry, as he inserted a *ranya* or osier-withy into his basket, and deftly twined it like a serpent to right and left, and almost as rapidly. Now a *slang* means, among divers things, a hawker's licence.

"I'm glad to hear it," I remarked. There was deep sincerity in this reply, as I had more than once contributed to the fees for the aforesaid *slangs*, which somehow or other were invariably refused to the applicant. At last, however, the slangs came; and his two boys, provided with them (at ten shillings per head), were now, in their sphere of life, in the position of young men who had received an education or been amply established in business, and were gifted with all that could be expected from a doting father. In its way this bit of intelligence meant as much to the basketmaker as, "Have you heard that young Fitz-Grubber has just got the double-first at Oxford?" or, "Do you know that old Cheshire has managed that appointment in India for his boy?--splendid independence, isn't it?" And I was shrewdly suspected by my audience, as the question implied, that I had had a hand in expanding this magnificent opening for the two fortunate young men.

"***Dick adoi***!" cried one, pointing up the river. "Look there at Jim!"

I looked and saw a young man far off, shirking along the path by the river, close to the hedge.

"He thinks you're a ***gav-mush***," observed Henry; "and he's got some sticks, an' is tryin' to hide them 'cause he daren't throw 'em away. Oh, aint he scared?"

It was a pleasing spectacle to see the demi-Gipsy coming in with his poor little green sticks, worth perhaps a halfpenny, and such as no living farmer in all North America would have grudged a cartload of to anybody. Droll as it really seemed, the sight touched me while I laughed. Oh, if charity covereth a multitude of sins, what should not poverty do? I care not through which door it comes--nay, be it by the very portal of Vice herself--when sad and shivering poverty stands before me in humble form, I can only forgive and forget. And this child-theft was to obtain the means of work after all. And if you ask me why I did not at once proceed to the next magistrate and denounce the criminal, I can only throw myself for excuse on the illustrious example of George the Fourth, head of Church and State, who once in society saw a pickpocket remove from a gentleman's fob his gold watch, winking at the king as he did so. "Of course I couldn't say anything," remarked the good-natured monarch, "for the rascal took me into his confidence."

Jim walked into camp amid mild chaff, to be greeted in Rommany by the suspected policeman, and to accept a glass of the ale, which had rained as it were from heaven into this happy family. These basketmakers were not real Gipsies, but ***churdi*** or half-bloods, though they spoke with scorn of the two chair-menders, who, working by themselves at the extremity of the tented town (and excluded from a share in the beer), seemed to be a sort of pariahs unto these higher casters.

I should mention, ***en passant***, that when the beer-bearer of the camp was sent for the three pots, he was told to "go over to Bill and borrow his two-gallon jug-- and be very careful not to let him find out what it was for." I must confess that I thought this was deeply unjust to the imposed-upon and beerless William; but it was another case of confidence, and he who sits among Gipsies by hedgerows green must not be over-particular. ***Il faut heurler avec les loups***. "Ain't it wrong to steal dese here chickens?" asked a negro who was seized with scruples while helping to rob a hen-roost. "Dat, Cuff, am a great moral question, an' we haint got time to discuss it--so jist hand down anoder pullet."

I found that Henry had much curious knowledge as to old Rommany ways, though he spoke with little respect of the Gipsy of the olden time, who, as he declared, thought all he needed in life was to get a row of silver buttons on his coat, a pair of high boots on his feet, and therewith-- *basta*! He had evidently met at one time with Mr George Borrow, as appeared by his accurate description of that gentleman's appearance, though he did not know his name. "Ah! he could talk the jib first-rateus," remarked my informant; "and he says to me, 'Bless you! you've all of you forgotten the real Gipsy language, and don't know anything about it at all.' Do you know Old Frank?" he suddenly inquired.

"Avo," I replied. "He's the man who has been twice in America."

"But d'ye know how rich he is? He's got money in bank. And when a man gets money in bank, *I* say there is somethin' in it. An' how do you suppose he made that money?" he inquired, with the air of one who is about to "come down with a stunner." "He did it *a-dukkerin*'." {171} But he pronounced the word *durkerin*'; and I, detecting at once, as I thought, an affinity with the German "turkewava," paused and stared, lost in thought. My pause was set down to amazement, and the Ancient Henry repeated--

"Fact. By *durkerin*'. I don't wonder you're astonished. Tellin' fortunes just like a woman. It isn't every man who could do that. But I suppose you could," he continued, looking at me admiringly. "You know all the ways of the Gorgios, an' could talk to ladies, an' are up to high life; ah, you could make no end of money. Why don't you do it?"

Innocent Gipsy! was this thy idea of qualification for a seer and a reader of dark lore? What wouldst thou say could I pour into thy brain the contents of the scores of works on "occult nonsense," from Agrippa to Zadkiel, devoured with keen hunger in the days of my youth? Yes, in solemn sadness, out of the whole I have brought no powers of divination; and in it all found nothing so strange as the wondrous tongue in which we spoke. In this mystery called Life many ways have been proposed to me of alleviating its expenses; as, for instance, when the old professor earnestly commended that we two should obtain (I trust honestly) a donkey and a *rinkni juva*, who by telling fortunes should entirely contribute to our maintenance, and so wander cost-free, and *kost-frei* over merrie England. But I threw away the golden opportunity--ruthlessly rejected it--thereby incurring the scorn of all scientific philologists (none of whom, I trow, would have lost such a chance). It was for doing the same thing that Matthew Arnold immortalised a clerke of Oxenforde: though it may be that "since Elizabeth" such exploits have lost their prestige, as I knew of two students at the same university who a few years ago went off on a six weeks' lark with two Gipsy girls; but who, far from desiring to have the fact chronicled in immortal rhyme, were even much afraid lest it should get into the county newspaper!

Leaving the basketmakers (among whom I subsequently found a grand-daughter of the celebrated Gipsy Queen, Charlotte Stanley), I went up the river, and there, above the bridge, found, as if withdrawn in pride, two other tents, by one of which stood a very pretty little girl of seven or eight years with a younger brother. While talking to the children, their father approached leading a horse. I had never seen him before, but he welcomed me politely in Rommany, saying that I had been pointed out to him as the Rommany rye, and that his mother, who was proficient in their language, was very desirous of meeting me. He was one of the smiths--a Petulengro or Petulamengro, or master of the horse- shoe, a name familiar to all readers of Lavengro.

This man was a full Gipsy, but he spoke better English, as well as better Rommany, than his neighbours, and had far more refinement of manner. And singularly enough, he appeared to be simpler hearted and more unaffected, with less Gipsy trickery, and more of a disposition for honest labour. His brother and uncle were, indeed, hard at work among the masons in a new building not far off, though they lived like true Gipsies in a tent. Petulamengro, as the name is commonly given at the present day, was evidently very proud of his Rommany, and talked little else: but he could not speak it nearly so well nor so fluently as his mother, who was of "the old sort," and who was, I believe, sincerely delighted that her skill was appreciated by me. All Gipsies are quite aware that their language is very old and curious, but they very seldom meet with Gorgios who are familiar with the fact, and manifest an interest in it.

While engaged in conversation with this family, Petulamengro asked me if I had ever met in America with Mr ---, adding, "He is a brother-in-law of mine."

I confess that I was startled, for I had known the gentleman in question very well for many years. He is a man of considerable fortune, and nothing in his appearance indicates in the slightest degree any affinity with the Rommany. He is not the only real or partial Gipsy whom I know among the wealthy and highly cultivated, and it is with pleasure I declare that I have found them all eminently kind-hearted and hospitable.

It may be worth while to state, in this connection, that Gipsy blood intermingled with Anglo-Saxon when educated, generally results in intellectual and physical vigour. The English Gipsy has greatly changed from the Hindoo in becoming courageous, in fact, his pugnacity and pluck are too frequently carried to a fault.

My morning's call had brought me into contact with the three types of the Gipsy of the roads. Of the half-breeds, and especially of those who have only a very slight trace of the dark blood or **kalo ratt**, there are in Great Britain many thousands. Of the true stock there are now only a few hundreds. But all are "Rommany," and all have among themselves an "understanding" which separates them from the "Gorgios."

It is difficult to define what this understanding is--suffice it to say, that it keeps them all in many respects "peculiar," and gives them a feeling of free-masonry, and of guarding a social secret, long after they leave the roads and become highly reputable members of society. But they have a secret, and no one can know them who has not penetrated it.

* * * *

One day I mentioned to my old Rommany, what Mr Borrow has said, that no English Gipsy knows the word for a leaf, or **patrin**. He admitted that it was true; but after considering the subject deeply, and dividing the deliberations between his pipe and a little wooden bear on the table--his regular oracle and friend--he suddenly burst forth in the following beautiful illustration of philology by theology:--

"Rya, I pens you the purodirus lav for a leaf--an' that's a **holluf**. (Don't you jin that the holluf was the firstus leaf? so holluf must be the Rommany lav, sense Rommanis is the purodirest jib o' saw.) For when the first mush was kaired an' created in the tem adree--and that was the boro Duvel himself, I expect--an' annered the tem apre, he was in the bero, an' didn't jin if there was any puvius about, so he bitchered the chillico avree. An' the chillico was a dove, 'cause dove-us is like Duvel, an' pash o' the Duvel an' Duvel's chillico. So the dove mukkered avree an' jalled round the tem till he latchered the puvius; for when he dickered a tan an' lelled a holluf-leaf, he jinned there was a tem, an' hatched the holluf apopli to his Duvel. An' when yuv's Duvel jinned there was a tem, he kaired bitti tiknos an' foki for the tem--an' I don't jin no more of it. Kekoomi. An' that is a wery tidy little story of the leaf, and it sikkers that the holluf was the first leaf. Tacho."

"Sir, I will tell you the oldest word for a leaf--and that is an olive. (Don't you know that the olive was the first leaf? so olive must be the Rommany word, since Rommanis is the oldest language of all.) For when the first man was made and created in the world--and that was the great God himself, I expect--and brought the land out, he was in the ship, and didn't know if there was any earth about him, so he sent the bird out. And the bird was a dove, because ***dove*** is like ***Duvel*** (God), and half God and God's bird. So the dove flew away and went around the world till he found the earth; for when he saw a place and took an olive-leaf, he knew there was a country (land), and took the olive-leaf back to his Lord. And when his Lord knew there was land, he made little children and people for it--and I don't know anything more about it. And that is a very tidy little story of the leaf, and it shows that the olive was the first leaf."

Being gratified at my noting down this original narrative from his own lips, my excellent old friend informed me, with cheerfulness not unmingled with the dignified pride characteristic of erudition, and of the possession of deep and darksome lore, that he also knew the story of Samson. And thus spake he:--

"Samson was a boro mush, wery hunnalo an' tatto at koorin', so that he nashered saw the mushis avree, an' they were atrash o' lester. He was so surrelo that yeckorus when he poggered avree a ker, an' it had a boro sasterni wuder, he just pet it apre his dumo, an' hookered it avree, an' jalled kerri an' bikin'd it.

"Yeck divvus he lelled some weshni juckals, an' pandered yagni-trushnees to their poris and mukked 'em jal. And they nashered avree like puro bengis, sig in the sala, when sar the mushis were sutto, 'unsa parl the giv puvius, and hotchered sar the giv.

"Then the krallis bitchered his mushis to lel Samson, but he koshered 'em, an' pash mored the tat of 'em; they couldn't kurry him, and he sillered 'em to praster for their miraben. An' 'cause they couldn't serber him a koorin', they kaired it sidd pre the chingerben drum. Now Samson was a seehiatty mush, wery cammoben to the juvas, so they got a wery rinkeni chi to kutter an' kuzzer him. So yuv welled a laki to a worretty tan, an' she hocussed him with drab till yuv was pilfry o' sutto, an his sherro hungered hooper side a lacker; an' when yuv was selvered, the mushis welled and chinned his ballos apre an' chivved him adree the sturaben.

"An' yeck divvus the foki hitchered him avree the sturaben to kair pyass for 'em. And as they were gillerin' and huljerin' him, Samson chivved his wasters kettenus the boro chongurs of the sturaben, and bongered his kokerus adree, an sar the ker pet a lay with a boro gudli, an' sar the pooro mushis were mullered an' the ker poggered to bitti cutters."

"Samson was a great man, very fierce and expert at fighting, so that he drove all men away, and they were afraid of him. He was so strong that once when he broke into a house, and it had a great iron door, he just put it on his back, and carried it away and went home and sold it.

"One day he caught some foxes, and tied firebrands to their tails and let them go. And they ran away like old devils, early in the morning, when all the people were asleep, across the field, and burned all the wheat.

"Then the king sent his men to take Samson, but he hurt them, and half killed the whole of them; they could not injure him, and he compelled them to run for life. And because they could not capture him by fighting, they did it otherwise by an opposite way. Now Samson was a man full of life, very fond of the girls, so they got a very pretty woman to cajole and coax him. And he went with her to a lonely house, and she 'hocussed' him with poison till he was heavy with sleep, and his head drooped by her side; and when he was poisoned, the people came and cut his hair off and threw him into prison.

"And one day the people dragged him out of prison to make sport for them. And as they were making fun of him and teasing him, Samson threw his hands around the great pillars of the prison, and bowed himself in, and all the house fell down with a great noise, and all the poor men were killed and the house broken to small pieces.

"And so he died."

"Do you know what the judgment day is, Puro?"

"Avo, rya. The judgment day is when you ***soves alay*** (go in sleep, or dream away) to the boro Duvel."

I reflected long on this reply of the untutored Rommany. I had often thought that the deepest and most beautiful phrase in all Tennyson's poems was that in which the impassioned lover promised his mistress to love her after death, ever on "into the dream beyond." And here I had the same thought as beautifully expressed by an old Gipsy, who, he declared, for two months hadn't seen three nights when he wasn't as drunk as four fiddlers. And the same might have been said of Carolan, the Irish bard, who lived in poetry and died in whisky.

The soul sleeping or dreaming away to God suggested an inquiry into the Gipsy idea of the nature of spirits.

"You believe in ***mullos*** (ghosts), Puro. Can everybody see them, I wonder?"

"Avo, rya, avo. Every mush can dick mullos if it's their cammoben to be dick-dus. But 'dusta critters can dick mullos whether the mullos kaum it or kek. There's grais an' mylas can dick mullos by the ratti; an' yeckorus I had a grai that was trasher 'dree a tem langs the rikkorus of a drum, pash a boro park where a mush had been mullered. He prastered a mee pauli, but pash a cheirus he welled apopli to the wardos. A chinned jucko or a wixen can hunt mullos. Avali, they chase sperits just the sim as anything 'dree the world--dan'r 'em, koor 'em, chinger 'em--'cause the dogs can't be dukkered by mullos."

In English: "Yes, sir, yes. Every man can see ghosts if it is their will to be seen. But many creatures can see ghosts whether the ghosts wish it or not. There are horses and asses (which) can see ghosts by the night; and once I had a horse that was frightened in a place by the side of a road, near a great park where a man had been murdered. He ran a mile behind, but after a while came back to the waggons. A cut (castrated) dog or a vixen can hunt ghosts. Yes, they chase spirits just the same as anything in the world--bite 'em, fight 'em, tear 'em--because dogs cannot be hurt by ghosts."

"Dogs," I replied, "sometimes hunt men as well as ghosts."

"Avo; but men can fool the juckals avree, and men too, and mullos can't."

"How do they kair it?"

"If a choramengro kaums to chore a covva when the snow is apre the puvius, he jals yeck piro, palewavescro. If you chiv tutes piros pal-o- the-waver--your kusto piro kaired bongo, jallin' with it a rikkorus, an' the waver piro straightus--your patteran'll dick as if a bongo-herroed mush had been apre the puvius. (I jinned a mush yeckorus that had a dui chokkas kaired with the dui tachabens kaired bongo, to jal a-chorin' with.) But if you're pallered by juckals, and pet lully dantymengro adree the chokkas, it'll dukker the sunaben of the juckos.

"An' if you chiv lully dantymengro where juckos kair panny, a'ter they soom it they won't jal adoi chichi no moreus, an' won't mutter in dovo tan, and you can keep it cleanus."

That is, "If a thief wants to steal a thing when the snow is on the ground, he goes with one foot behind the other. If you put your feet one behind the other-- your right foot twisted, going with it to one side, and the other foot straight--your trail will look as if a crooked-legged man had been on the ground. (I knew a man once that had a pair of shoes made with the two heels reversed, to go a-thieving with.) But if you are followed by dogs, and put red pepper in your shoes, it will spoil the scent of the dogs.

"And if you throw red pepper where dogs make water, they will not go there any more after they smell it, and you can keep it clean."

"Well," I replied, "I see that a great many things can be learned from the Gipsies. Tell me, now, when you wanted a night's lodging did you ever go to a union?"

"Kek, rya; the tramps that jal langs the drum an' mang at the unions are kek Rommany chals. The Rommany never kair dovo--they'd sooner besh in the bavol puv firstus. We'd putch the farming rye for mukkaben to hatch the ratti adree the granja, but we'd sooner suv under the bor in the bishnoo than jal adree the chuv- veny-ker. The Rommany chals aint sim to tramps, for they've got a different drum into 'em."

In English: "No, sir; the tramps that go along the road and beg at the unions are not Gipsies. The Rommany never do that--they'd sooner stay in the open field (literally, air-field). We would ask the farmer for leave to stop the night in the barn, but we'd sooner sleep under the hedge in the rain than go in the poorhouse. Gipsies are not like tramps, for they have a different *way*."

The reader who will reflect on the extreme misery and suffering incident upon sleeping in the open air, or in a very scanty tent, during the winter in England, and in cold rains, will appreciate the amount of manly pride necessary to sustain the Gipsies in thus avoiding the union. That the wandering Rommany can live at all is indeed wonderful, since not only are all other human beings less exposed to suffering than many of them, but even foxes and rabbits are better protected in their holes from storms and frost. The Indians of North America have, without exception, better tents; in fact, one of the last Gipsy *tans* which I visited was merely a bit of ragged canvas, so small that it could only cover the upper portion of the bodies of the man and his wife who slept in it. Where and how they packed their two children I cannot understand.

The impunity with which any fact might be published in English Rommany, with the certainty that hardly a soul in England not of the blood could understand it, is curiously illustrated by an incident which came within my knowledge. The reader is probably aware that there appear occasionally in the "Agony" column of the *Times* (or in that devoted to "personal" advertisements) certain sentences apparently written in some very strange foreign tongue, but which the better informed are aware are made by transposing letters according to the rules of cryptography or secret writing. Now it is estimated that there are in Great Britain at least one thousand lovers of occult lore and quaint curiosa, decipherers of rebuses and adorers of anagrams, who, when one of these delightful puzzles appears in the *Times*, set themselves down and know no rest until it is unpuzzled and made clear, being stimulated in the pursuit by the delightful consciousness that they are exploring the path of somebody's secret, which somebody would be very sorry to have made known.

Such an advertisement appeared one day, and a friend of mine, who had a genius for that sort of thing, sat himself down early one Saturday morning to decipher it.

First of all he ascertained which letter occurred most frequently in the advertisement, for this must be the letter *e* according to rules made and provided by the great Edgar A. Poe, the American poet-cryptographer. But to reveal the secret in full, I may as well say, dear reader, that you must take printers' type in their cases, ***and follow the proportions according to the size of the boxes***. By doing this you cannot fail to unrip the seam of any of these transmutations.

But, alas! this cock would not fight--it was a dead bird in the pit. My friend at once apprehended that he had to deal with an old hand--one of those aggravating fellows who are up to cryp--a man who can write a sentence, and be capable of leaving the letter *e* entirely out. For there *are* people who will do this.

So he went to work afresh upon now hypotheses, and pleasantly the hours fled by. Quires of paper were exhausted; he worked all day and all the evening with no result. That it was not in a foreign language my friend was well assured.

> "For well hee knows the Latine and the Dutche;   Of Fraunce and Toscanie he hath a touche."

Russian is familiar to him, and Arabic would not have been an unknown quantity. So he began again with the next day, and had been breaking the Sabbath until four o'clock in the afternoon, when I entered, and the mystic advertisement was submitted to me. I glanced at it, and at once read it into English, though as I read the smile at my friend's lost labour vanished in a sense of sympathy for what the writer must have suffered. It was as follows, omitting names:--

> "MANDY jins of --- ---. Patsa mandy, te bitcha lav ki tu shan. Opray   minno lav, mandy'l kek pukka til tute muks a mandi. Tute's di's see   se welni poggado. Shom atrash tuti dad'l jal divio. Yov'l fordel   sor. For miduvel's kom, muk lesti shoon choomani."

In English: "I know of ---. Trust me, and send word where you are. On my word, I will not tell till you give me leave. Your mother's heart is wellnigh broken. I am afraid your father will go mad. He will forgive all. For God's sake, let him know something."

This was sad enough, and the language in which it was written is good English Rommany. I would only state in addition, that I found that in the very house in which I was living, and at the same time, a lady had spent three days in vainly endeavouring to ascertain the meaning of these sentences.

It is possible that many Gipsies, be they of high or low degree, in society or out of it, may not be pleased at my publishing a book of their language, and revealing so much of what they fondly cherish as a secret. They need be under no apprehension, since I doubt very much whether, even with its aid, a dozen persons living will seriously undertake to study it--and of this dozen there is not one who will not be a philologist; and such students are generally aware that there are copious vocabularies of all the other Gipsy dialects of Europe easy to obtain from any bookseller. Had my friend used the works of Pott or Paspati, Ascoli or Grellman, he would have found it an easy thing to translate this advertisement. The truth simply is, that for *scholars* there is not a single secret or hidden word in English Gipsy or in any other Rommany dialect, and none except scholars will take pains to acquire it. Any man who wished to learn sufficient Gipsy to maintain a conversation, and thereby learn all the language, could easily have done so half a century ago from the vocabularies published by Bright and other writers. A secret which has been for fifty years published in very practical detail in fifty books, is indeed a *secret de Ponchinelle*.

I have been asked scores of times, "Have the Gipsies an alphabet of their own? have they grammars of their language, dictionaries, or books?" Of course my answer was in the negative. I have heard of vocabularies in use among crypto-Rommanies, or those who having risen from the roads live a secret life, so to speak, but I have never seen one. But they have songs; and one day I was told that in my neighbourhood there lived a young Gipsy woman who was a poetess and made Rommany ballads. "She can't write," said my informant; "but her husband's a *Gorgio*, and he can. If you want them, I'll get you some." The offer was of course accepted, and the Gipsy dame, flattered by the request, sent me the following. The lyric is without rhyme, but, as sung, not without rhythm.

"GILLI OF A RUMMANY JUVA.

"Die at the gargers (Gorgios),
The gargers round mandy!
Trying to lel my meripon,
My meripon (meripen) away.

I will care (kair) up to my chungs (chongs),
Up to my chungs in Rat,
All for my happy Racler (raklo).

My mush is lelled to sturribon (staripen),
To sturribon, to sturribon;
Mymush is lelled to sturribon,

To the Tan where mandy gins (jins)."

TRANSLATION.

"Look at the Gorgios, the Gorgios around me! trying to take my life away.

"I will wade up to my knees in blood, all for my happy boy.

"My husband is taken to prison, to prison, to prison; my husband is taken to prison, to the place of which I know."

CHAPTER X. GIPSIES IN EGYPT.

Difficulty of obtaining Information.--The Khedive on the Gipsies.--Mr Edward Elias.--Mahomet introduces me to the Gipsies.--They call themselves Tataren.--The Rhagarin or Gipsies at Boulac.--Cophts.--Herr Seetzen on Egyptian Gipsies.--The Gipsy with the Monkey in Cairo.--Street- cries of the Gipsy Women in Egypt. Captain Newbold on the Egyptian Gipsies.

Since writing the foregoing pages, and only a day or two after one of the incidents therein described, I went to Egypt, passing the winter in Cairo and on the Nile. While waiting in the city for the friend with whom I was to ascend the mysterious river, it naturally occurred to me, that as I was in the country which many people still believe is the original land of the Gipsies, it would be well worth my while to try to meet with some, if any were to be found.

It is remarkable, that notwithstanding my inquiries from many gentlemen, both native and foreign, including savans and beys, the only educated person I ever met in Egypt who was able to give me any information on the subject of its Gipsies was the Khedive or Viceroy himself, a fact which will not seem strange to those who are aware of the really wonderful extent of his knowledge of the country which he rules. I had been but a few days in Cairo when, at an interview with the Khedive, Mr Beardsley, the American Consul, by whom I was presented, mentioned to his Highness that I was interested in the subject of the Gipsies, upon which the Khedive said that there were in Egypt many people known as " *Rhagarin* " (Ghagarin), who were probably the same as the "Bohemiens" or Gipsies of Europe. His words were, as nearly as I can remember, as follows:--

"They are wanderers who live in tents, and are regarded with contempt even by the peasantry. Their women tell fortunes, tattoo, {189} and sell small-wares; the men work in iron (*quincaillerie*). They are all adroit thieves, and noted as such.

The men may sometimes be seen going around the country with monkeys; in fact, they appear to be in all respects the same people as the Gipsies of Europe."

This was all that I could learn for several days; for though there were Gipsies--or "Egypcians"--in Egypt, I had almost as much trouble to find them as Eilert Sundt had to discover their brethren in Norway. In speaking of the subject to Mr Edward Elias, a gentleman well known in Egypt, he most kindly undertook to secure the aid of the chief of police, who in turn had recourse to the Shekh of the Gipsies. But the Shekh I was told was not himself a Gipsy, and there were none of his subjects in Cairo. After a few days, three wanderers, supposed to be Rommany, were arrested; but on examination they proved to be ignorant of any language except Arabic. Their occupation was music and dancing "with a stick;" in fact, they were performers in those curious and extremely ancient Fescennine farces, or ***Atellanae***, which are depicted on ancient vases, and are still acted on the roads in Egypt as they were in Greece before the days of Thespis. Then I was informed that Gipsies were often encamped near the Pyramids, but research in this direction was equally fruitless.

Remembering what his Highness had told me, that Gipsies went about exhibiting monkeys, I one day, on meeting a man bearing an ape, endeavoured to enter into conversation with him. Those who know Cairo can imagine with what result! In an instant we were surrounded by fifty natives of the lower class, jabbering, jeering, screaming, and begging--all intent, as it verily seemed, on defeating my object. I gave the monkey-bearer money; instead of thanking me, he simply clamoured for more, while the mob became intolerable, so that I was glad to make my escape.

At last I was successful. I had frequently employed as donkey-driver an intelligent and well-behaved man named Mahomet, who spoke English well, and who was familiar with the byways of Cairo. On asking him if he could show me any Rhagarin, he replied that every Saturday there was a fair or market held at Boulac, where I would be sure to meet with women of the tribe. The men, I was told, seldom ventured into the city, because they were subject to much insult and ill-treatment from the common people. On the day appointed I rode to the market, which was extremely interesting. There were thousands of blue-shirted and red-tarbouched or white-turbaned Egyptians, buying or selling, or else merely amusing themselves; dealers in sugar-cane, pipe-pedlars, and vendors of rosaries; jugglers and minstrels. At last we came to a middle-aged woman seated on the ground behind a basket containing beads, glass armlets, and similar trinkets. She was dressed like any Arab woman of the lower class, but was not veiled, and on her chin blue lines were tattooed. Her features and whole expression were, however, evidently Gipsy.

I spoke to her in Rommany, using such words as would have been intelligible to any of the race in England, Germany, or Turkey; but she did not understand me, and declared that she could speak nothing but Arabic. At my request Mahomet explained to her that I had travelled from a distant country in "Orobba," where there were many Rhagarin who declared that their fathers came from Egypt, and that I wished to know if any in the latter country could speak the old language. She replied that the Rhagarin of "Montesinos" could still speak it, but that her people in Egypt had lost the tongue. Mahomet declared that Montesinos meant Mount Sinai or Syria. I then asked her if the Rhagarin had no peculiar name for themselves, and she replied, "Yes, we call ourselves Tataren."

This was at least satisfactory. All over Southern Germany and in Norway the Rommany are sailed Tataren; and though the word means Tartars, and is simply a misapplied term, it indicates a common race. The woman seemed to be very much gratified at the interest I manifested in her people. I gave her a double piastre, and asked for its value in blue-glass armlets. She gave me two pair, and as I turned to depart called me back, and with a good-natured smile handed me four more as a present. This generosity was very Gipsy-like, and very unlike the usual behaviour of any common Egyptian.

While on the Nile, I inquired of people in different towns if they had ever seen Gipsies where they lived, and was invariably answered in the negative. Remembering to have read in some book a statement that the Ghawazi or dancing-girls formed a tribe by themselves, and spoke a peculiar language, I asked an American who has lived for many years in Egypt if he thought they could be Gipsies. He replied that an English lady of title, who had also been for a long time in the country, had formed this opinion. But when I questioned dancing-girls myself, I found them quite ignorant of any language except Arabic, and knowing nothing relating to the Rommany. Two Ghawazi whom I saw had, indeed, the peculiarly brilliant eyes and general expression of Gipsies. The rest appeared to be Egyptian-Arab; and I found on inquiry that one of the latter had really been a peasant girl who till within seven months had worked in the fields, while two others were occupied alternately with field-work and dancing.

At the market in Boulac, Mahomet took me to a number of **Rhagarin**. They all resembled the one whom I have described, and were all occupied in selling exactly the same class of articles. They all differed slightly, as I thought, from the ordinary Egyptians in their appearance, and were decidedly unlike them, in being neither importunate for money nor disagreeable in their manners. But though they were certainly Gipsies, none of them would speak Rommany, and I doubt very much if they could have done so.

Bonaventura Vulcanius, who in 1597 first gave the world a specimen of Rommany in his curious book "De Literis et Lingua Getarum" (which specimen, by the way, on account of its rarity, I propose to republish in another work), believed that the Gipsies were Nubians; and others, following in his track, supposed they were really Cophtic Christians (Pott, "Die Zigeuner," &c., Halle, 1844, p. 5). And I must confess that this recurred forcibly to my memory when, at Minieh, in Egypt, I asked a Copht scribe if he were Muslim, and he replied, "*La*, *ana Gipti*" ("No, I am a Copht"), pronouncing the word *Gipti*, or Copht, so that it might readily be taken for "Gipsy." And learning that *romi* is the Cophtic for a man, I was again startled; and when I found *tema* (tem, land) and other Rommany words in ancient Egyptian (*vide* Brugsch, "Grammaire," &c.), it seemed as if there were still many mysteries to solve in this strange language.

Other writers long before me attempted to investigate Egyptian Gipsy, but with no satisfactory result. A German named Seetzen ascertained that there were Gipsies both in Egypt and Syria, and wrote (1806) on the subject a MS., which Pott ("Die Zigeuner," &c.) cites largely. Of these Roms he speaks as follows: "Gipsies are to be found in the entire Osmanli realm, from the limits of Hungary into Egypt. The Turks call them Tschinganih; but the Syrians and Egyptians, as well as themselves, *Nury*, in the plural *El Nauar*. It was on the 24th November 1806 when I visited a troop of them, encamped with their black tents in an olive grove, to the west side of Naplos. They were for the greater part of a dirty yellow complexion, with black hair, which hung down on the side from where it was parted in a short plait, and their lips are mulatto- like." (Seetzen subsequently remarks that their physiognomy is precisely like that of the modern Egyptians.) "The women had their under lips coloured dark blue, like female Bedouins, and a few eaten-in points around the mouth of like colour. They, and the boys also, wore earrings. They made sieves of horse-hair or of leather, iron nails, and similar small ironware, or mended kettles. They appear to be very poor, and the men go almost naked, unless the cold compels them to put on warmer clothing. The little boys ran about naked. Although both Christians and Mahometans declared that they buried their dead in remote hill corners, or burned them, they denied it, and declared they were good Mahometans, and as such buried their dead in Mahometan cemeteries." (This corresponds to their custom in Great Britain in the past generation, and the earnestness which they display at present to secure regular burial like Christians.) "But as their instruction is even more neglected than that of the Bedouins, their religious information is so limited that one may say of them, they have either no religion at all, or the simplest of all. As to wine, they are less strict than most Mahometans. They assured me that in Egypt there were many *Nury*."

The same writer obtained from one of these Syrian-Egyptian Gipsies a not inconsiderable vocabulary of their language, and says: "I find many Arabic, Turkish, and some Greek words in it; it appears to me, however, that they have borrowed from a fourth language, which was perhaps their mother-tongue, but which I cannot name, wanting dictionaries." The words which he gives appear to me to consist of Egyptian-Arabic, with its usual admixture from other sources, simply made into a gibberish, and sometimes with one word substituted for another to hide the meaning--the whole probably obtained through a dragoman, as is seen, for instance, when he gives the word *nisnaszeha*, a fox, and states that it is of unknown origin. The truth is, *nisnas* means a monkey, and, like most of Seetzen's "Nuri" words, is inflected with an *a* final, as if one should say "monkeyo." I have no doubt the Nauar may talk such a jargon; but I should not be astonished, either, if the Shekh who for a small pecuniary consideration eagerly aided Seetzen to note it down, had "sold" him with what certainly would appear to any Egyptian to be the real babble of the nursery. There are a very few Rommany words in this vocabulary, but then it should be remembered that there are some Arabic words in Rommany.

The street-cry of the Gipsy women in Cairo is [ARABIC TEXT which cannot be reproduced] " *Neduqq wanetahir*!" "We tattoo and circumcise!" a phrase which sufficiently indicates their calling. In the "Deutscher Dragoman" of Dr Philip Wolff, Leipzig, 1867, I find the following under the word Zigeuner:--

"Gipsy--in Egypt, Gagri" (pronounced more nearly 'Rh'agri), "plural **Gagar**; in Syria, **Newari**, plural **Nawar**. When they go about with monkeys, they are called **Kurudati**, from **kird**, ape. The Gipsies of Upper Egypt call themselves Saaideh-- *i.e.*, people from Said, or Upper Egypt (*vide* Kremer, i. 138-148). According to Von Gobineau, they are called in Syria Kurbati, [ARABIC TEXT which cannot be reproduced] (*vide* 'Zeitschrift der D. M. G.,' xi. 690)."

More than this of the Gipsies in Egypt the deponent sayeth not. He has interrogated the oracles, and they were dumb. That there are Roms in the land of Mizr his eyes have shown, but whether any of them can talk Rommany is to him as yet unknown.

* * * *

Since the foregoing was printed, I have found in the *Journal of the Royal Asiatic Society* (Vol. XVI., Part 2, 1856, p. 285), an article on The Gipsies in Egypt, by the late Captain Newbold, F.R.S., which gives much information on this mysterious subject. The Egyptian Gipsies, as Captain Newbold found, are extremely jealous and suspicious of any inquiry into their habits and mode of life, so that he had great difficulty in tracing them to their haunts, and inducing them to unreserved communication.

These Gipsies are divided into three kinds, the Helebis, Ghagars (Rhagarin), and Nuris or Nawer. Of the Rhagars there are sixteen thousand. The Helebi are most prosperous of all these, and their women, who are called Fehemis, are the only ones who practice fortune-telling and sorcery. The male Helebis are chiefly ostensible dealers in horses and cattle, but have a bad character for honesty. Some of them are to be found in every official department in Egypt, though not known to be Gipsies--(a statement which casts much light on the circumstance that neither the chief of police himself nor the Shekh of the Rhagarin, with all their alleged efforts, could find a single Gipsy for me). The Helebis look down on the Rhagarin, and do not suffer their daughters to intermarry with them, though they themselves marry Rhagarin girls. The Fehemi, or Helebi women, are noted for their chastity; the Rhagarin are not. The men of the Rhagarin are tinkers and blacksmiths, and sell cheap jewellery or instruments of iron and brass. Many of them are athletes, mountebanks, and monkey-exhibitors; the women are rope-dancers and musicians. They are divided into classes, bearing the names of Romani, Meddahin, Ghurradin, Barmeki (Barmecides), Waled Abu Tenna, Beit er Rafai, Hemmeli, &c. The Helebis and Rhagarin are distinctly different in their personal appearance from the other inhabitants of Egypt, having the eyes and expression peculiar to all Gipsies. Captain Newbold, in fact, assumes that any person "who remains in Egypt longer than the ordinary run of travellers, and roams about the streets and environs of the large towns, can hardly fail to notice the strange appearance of certain females, whose features at once distinguish them from the ordinary Fellah Arabs and Cophts of the country."

"The Nuris or Nawers are hereditary thieves, but are now (1856) employed as police and watchmen in the Pacha's country estates. In Egypt they intermarry with the Fellahin or Arabs of the soil, from whom, in physical appearance and dress, they can hardly be distinguished. Outwardly they profess Mohammedanism, and have little intercourse with the Helebis and Ghagars (or Rhagarin)."

Each of these tribes or classes speak a separate and distinct dialect or jargon. That of the Rhagarin most resembles the language spoken by the Kurbats, or Gipsies of Syria. "It seems to me probable," says Captain Newbold, "that the whole of these tribes had one common origin in India, or the adjacent countries on its Western frontier, and that the difference in the jargons they now speak is owing to their sojourn in the various countries through which they have passed. ***This is certain, that the Gipsies are strangers in the land of Egypt***."

I am not astonished, on examining the specimens of these three dialects given by Captain Newbold, with the important addition made by Mr W. Burckhardt Barker, that I could not converse with the Rhagarin. That of the Nawers does not contain a single word which would be recognised as Rommany, while those which occur in the other two jargons are, if not positively either few and far between, strangely distorted from the original. A great number are ordinary vulgar Arabic. It is very curious that while in England such a remarkably large proportion of Hindustani words have been preserved, they have been lost in the East, in countries comparatively near the fatherland--India.

I would, in conclusion to this work, remark that numbers of Rommany words, which are set down by philologists as belonging to Greek, Slavonian, and other languages, were originally Hindu, and have only changed their form a little because the wanderers found a resemblance to the old word in a new one. I am also satisfied that much may be learned as to the origin of these words from a familiar acquaintance with the vulgar dialects of Persia, and such words as are not put down in dictionaries, owing to their provincial character. I have found, on questioning a Persian gentleman, that he knew the meaning of many Rommany words from their resemblance to vulgar Persian, though they were not in the Persian dictionary which I used.

ROMMANI GUDLI; OR, GIPSY STORIES AND FABLES.

The Gipsy to whom I was chiefly indebted for the material of this book frequently narrated to me the *Gudli* or small stories current among his people, and being a man of active, though child-like imagination, often invented others of a similar character. Sometimes an incident or saying would suggest to me the outline of a narrative, upon which he would eagerly take it up, and readily complete the tale. But if I helped him sometimes to evolve from a hint, a phrase, or a fact, something like a picture, it was always the Gipsy who gave it Rommany characteristics and conferred colour. It was often very difficult for him to distinctly recall an old story or clearly develop anything of the kind, whether it involved an effort of memory or of the imagination, and here he required aid. I have never in my life met with any man whose mind combined so much simplicity, cunning, and grotesque fancy, with such an entire incapacity to appreciate either humour or "poetry" as expressed in the ordinary language of culture. The metre and rhyme of the simplest ballad made it unintelligible to him, and I was obliged to repeat such poetry several times before he could comprehend it. Yet he would, while I was otherwise occupied than with him, address to his favourite wooden image of a little bear on the chimneypiece, grotesque soliloquies which would have delighted a Hoffman, or conduct with it dialogues which often startled me. With more education, he would have become a Rommany Bid- pai; and since India is the fatherland of the fable, he may have derived his peculiar faculty for turning morals and adorning tales legitimately from that source.

I may state that those stories, which were made entirely; as a few were; or in part, by my assistant and myself, were afterwards received with approbation by ordinary Gipsies as being thoroughly Rommany. As to the *language* of the stories, it is all literally and faithfully that of a Gipsy, word by word, written down as he uttered it, when, after we had got a *gudlo* into shape, he told it finally over, which he invariably did with great eagerness, ending with an improvised moral.

GUDLO I. HOW A GIPSY SAVED A CHILD'S LIFE BY BREAKING A WINDOW.

'Pre yeck divvus (or yeckorus) a Rommany chal was kairin' pyass with the koshters, an' he wussered a kosh 'pre the hev of a boro ker an' poggered it. Welled the prastramengro and penned, "Tu must pooker (or pessur) for the glass." But when they jawed adree the ker, they lastered the kosh had mullered a divio juckal that was jawan' to dant the chavo. So the rani del the Rommany chal a sonnakai ora an' a fino gry.

But yeck koshter that poggers a hev doesn't muller a juckal.

TRANSLATION.

On a day (or once) a Gipsy was playing at cockshy, and he threw a stick through the window of a great house and broke the glass. Came the policeman and said, "You must answer (or pay) for the glass." But when they went into the house, they found the stick had killed a mad dog that was going to bite the child (boy). So the lady gave the Gipsy a gold watch and a good horse.

But every stick that breaks a window does not kill a dog.

GUDLO II. THE GIPSY STORY OF THE BIRD AND THE HEDGEHOG.

'Pre yeck divvus a hotchewitchi dicked a chillico adree the puv, and the chillico pukkered lesco, "Mor jal pauli by the kushto wastus, or the hunters' graias will chiv tute adree the chick, mullo; an' if you jal the waver rikk by the bongo wast, dovo's a Rommany tan adoi, and the Rommany chals will haw tute." Penned the hotchewitchi, "I'd rather jal with the Rommany chals, an' be hawed by foki that kaum mandy, than be pirraben apre by chals that dick kaulo apre mandy."

It's kushtier for a tacho Rom to be mullered by a Rommany pal than to be nashered by the Gorgios.

TRANSLATION.

On a day a hedgehog met a bird in the field, and the bird told him, "Do not go around by the right hand, or the hunters' horses will trample you dead in the dirt; and if you go around by the left hand, there's a Gipsy tent, and the Gipsies will eat you." Said the hedgehog, "I'd rather go with the Gipsies, and be eaten by folk that like me, than be trampled on by people that despise (literally, look black upon) me."

It is better for a real Gipsy to be killed by a Gipsy brother than to be hung by Gorgios.

GUDLO III. A STORY OF A FORTUNE-TELLER.

Yeckorus a tano Gorgio chivved apre a shubo an' jalled to a puri Rommany dye to get dukkered. And she pookered lester, "Tute'll rummorben a Fair Man with kauli yakkas." Then the raklo delled laki yeck shukkori an' penned, "If this shukkori was as boro as the hockaben tute pukkered mandy, tute might porder sar the bongo tem with rupp." But, hatch a wongish!--maybe in a divvus, maybe in a curricus, maybe a dood, maybe a besh, maybe waver divvus, he rummorbend a rakli by the nav of Fair Man, and her yakkas were as kaulo as miri juva's.

There's always dui rikk to a dukkerben.

TRANSLATION.

Once a little Gorgio put on a woman's gown and went to an old Gipsy mother to have his fortune told. And she told him, "You'll marry a Fair Man with black eyes." Then the young man gave her a sixpence and said, "If this sixpence were as big as the lie you told me, you could fill all hell with silver." But, stop a bit! after a while--maybe in a week, maybe a month, maybe in a year, maybe the other day--he married a girl by the name of Fair Man, and her eyes were as black as my sweetheart's.

There are always two sides to a prediction.

GUDLO IV. HOW THE ROYSTON ROOK DECEIVED THE ROOKS AND PIGEONS.

'Pre yeck divvus a Royston rookus jalled mongin the kaulo chiriclos, an' they putched (pootschered) him, "Where did tute chore tiro pauno chukko?" And yuv pookered, "Mandy chored it from a biksherro of a pigeon." Then he jalled a-men the pigeons an' penned, "Sarishan, pals?" And they putched lesti, "Where did tute lel akovo kauli rokamyas te byascros?" And yuv penned, "Mandy chored 'em from those wafri mushis the rookuses."

Pash-ratis pen their kokeros for Gorgios mongin Gorgios, and for Rommany mongin Rommany chals.

TRANSLATION.

On a day a Royston rook {206} went among the crows (black birds), and they asked him, "Where did you steal your white coat?" And he told (them), "I stole it from a fool of a pigeon." Then he went among the pigeons and said, "How are you, brothers?" And they asked him, "Where did you get those black trousers and sleeves?" And he said, "I stole 'em from those wretches the rooks."

Half-breeds call themselves Gorgio among Gorgios, and Gipsy among Gipsies.

GUDLO V. THE GIPSY'S STORY OF THE GORGIO AND THE ROMMANY CHAL.

Once 'pre a chairus (or chyrus) a Gorgio penned to a Rommany chal, "Why does tute always jal about the tem ajaw? There's no kushtoben in what don't hatch acai." Penned the Rommany chal, "Sikker mandy tute's wongur!" And yuv sikkered him a cutter (cotter?), a bar, a pash-bar, a pash-cutter, a pange-cullo (caulor?) bittus, a pash-krooner (korauna), a dui-cullos bittus, a trin-mushi, a shuckori, a stor'oras, a trin'oras, a dui'oras, a haura, a poshero, a lulli, a pash-lulli. Penned the Rommany chal, "Acovo's sar wafri wongur." "Kek," penned the Gorgio; "se sar kushto an' kirus. Chiv it adree tute's wast and shoon it ringus." "Avo," penned the Rommany chal. "Tute pookered mandy that only wafri covvas keep jallin', te 'covo wongur has jalled sar 'pre the 'tem adusta timei (or timey)."

Sar mushis aren't all sim ta rukers (rukkers.) Some must pirraben, and can't besh't a lay.

TRANSLATION.

Once upon a time a Gorgio said to a Gipsy, "Why do you always go about the country so? There is 'no good' in what does not rest (literally, stop here)." Said the Gipsy, "Show me your money!" And he showed him a guinea, a sovereign, a half-sovereign, a half-guinea, a five-shilling piece, a half-crown, a two-shilling piece, a shilling, a sixpence, a fourpenny piece, a threepence, a twopence, a penny, a half-penny, a farthing, a half-farthing. Said the Gipsy, "This is all bad money." "No," said the other man; "it is all good and sound. Toss it in your hand and hear it ring!" "Yes," replied the Gipsy. "You told me that only bad things ***keep going***, and this money has gone all over the country many a time."

All men are not like trees. Some must travel, and cannot keep still.

GUDLO VI. HOW THE GIPSY BRIBED THE POLICEMAN.

Once apre a chairus a Rommany chal chored a rani chillico (or chiriclo), and then jalled atut a prastramengro 'pre the drum. "Where did tute chore adovo rani?" putchered the prastramengro. "It's kek rani; it's a pauno rani that I kinned 'dree the gav to del tute." "Tacho," penned the prastramengro, "it's the kushtiest pauno rani mandy ever dickdus. Ki did tute kin it?"

Avali, many's the chairus mandy's tippered a trinmushi to a prastramengro ta mukk mandy hatch my tan with the chavvis.

TRANSLATION.

Once on a time a Gipsy stole a turkey, and then met a policeman on the road. "Where did you steal that turkey?" asked the policeman. "It's no turkey; it's a goose that I bought in the town to give you." "Fact," said the policeman, "it *is* the finest goose I ever saw. Where *did* you buy it?"

Yes, many's the time I have given a shilling (three fourpence) to a policeman to let me pitch my tent with the children. {209}

GUDLO VII. HOW A GIPSY LOST THREEPENCE.

Yeckorus a choro mush besht a lay ta kair trin horras-worth o' peggi for a masengro. There jessed alang's a rye, who penned, "Tool my gry, an' I'll del tute a shukori." While he tooled the gry a rani pookered him, "Rikker this trushni to my ker, an' I'll del tute a trin grushi." So he lelled a chavo to tool the gry, and pookered lester, "Tute shall get pash the wongur." Well, as yuv was rikkinin' the trushnee an' siggerin burry ora bender the drum, he dicked a rye, who penned, "If tute'll jaw to the ker and hatch minni's juckal ta mandy, mi'll del tute a pash-korauna." So he got a waver chavo to rikker the trushnee for pash the wongur, whilst he jalled for the juckal. Wellin' alangus, he dicked a barvelo givescro, who penned, "'Avacai an' husker mandy to lel my guruvni (*gruvni*) avree the ditch, and I'll del you pange cullos" (caulos). So he lelled it. But at the kunsus of the divvus, sa yuv sus kennin apre sustis wongurs, he penned, "How wafro it is mandy nashered the trinoras I might have lelled for the mass-koshters!"

A mush must always pet the giv in the puv before he can chin the harvest.

TRANSLATION.

Once a poor man sat down to make threepence-worth of skewers {210} for a butcher. There came along a gentleman, who said, "Hold my horse, and I'll give you a sixpence." While he held the horse a lady said to him, "Carry this basket to my house, and I'll give you a shilling." So he got a boy to hold the horse, and said to him, "You shall have half the money." Well, as he was carrying the basket and hurrying along fast across the road he saw a gentleman, who said, "If you'll go to the house and bring my dog to me, I will give you half-a-crown." So he got another boy to carry the basket for half the money, while he went for the dog. Going along, he saw a rich farmer, who said, "Come and help me here to get my cow out of the ditch, and I'll give you five shillings." So he got it. But at the end of the day, when he was counting his money, he said, "What a pity it is I lost the threepence I might have got for the skewers!" (literally, meat-woods.)

A man must always put the grain in the ground before he can cut the harvest.

GUDLO VIII. THE STORY OF THE GIPSY'S DOG.

'Pre yeck divvus a choro mush had a juckal that used to chore covvas and hakker them to the ker for his mush--mass, wongur, horas, and rooys. A rye kinned the juckal, an' kaired boot dusta wongur by sikkerin' the juckal at wellgooras.

Where barvelo mushis can kair wongur tacho, chori mushis have to loure.

TRANSLATION.

On a day a poor man had a dog that used to steal things and carry them home for his master--meat, money, watches, and spoons. A gentleman bought the dog, and made a great deal of money by showing him at fairs.

Where rich men can make money honestly, poor men have to steal.

GUDLO IX. A STORY OF THE PRIZE-FIGHTER AND THE GENTLEMAN.

'Pre yeck chairus a cooromengro was to coor, and a rye rakkered him, "Will tute mukk your kokero be koored for twenty bar?" Penned the cooromengro, "Will tute mukk mandy pogger your herry for a hundred bar?" "Kek," penned the rye; "for if I did, mandy'd never pirro kushto ajaw." "And if I nashered a kooraben," penned the engro, "mandy'd never praster kekoomi."

Kammoben is kushtier than wongur.

TRANSLATION.

On a time a prize-fighter was to fight, and a gentleman asked him, "Will you sell the fight" (*i.e.*, let yourself be beaten) "for twenty pounds?" Said the prize-fighter, "Will you let me break your leg for a hundred pounds?" "No," said the gentleman; "for if I did, I should never walk well again." "And if I lost a fight," said the prize-fighter (literally, master, doer), "I could never 'run' again."

Credit is better than money.

GUDLO X. OF THE GENTLEMAN AND THE OLD GIPSY WOMAN.

Pre yeck chairus a Rommany dye adree the wellgooro rakkered a rye to del laker trin mushi for kushto bak. An' he del it, an' putchered laki, "If I bitcher my wongur a-mukkerin' 'pre the graias, ki'll manni's bak be?" "My fino rye," she penned, "the bak'll be a collos-worth with mandy and my chavvis."

Bak that's pessured for is saw (sar) adoi.

TRANSLATION.

On a time a Gipsy mother at the fair asked a gentleman to give her a shilling for luck. And he gave it, and asked her, "If I lose my money a- betting on the horses, where will my luck be?" "My fine gentleman," she said, "the luck will be a shilling's worth with me and my children."

Luck that is paid for is always somewhere (literally, there).

GUDLO XI. THE GIPSY TELLS OF THE CAT AND THE HARE.

Yeckorus the matchka jalled to dick her kako's chavo the kanengro. An' there welled a huntingmush, an' the matchka taddied up the choomber, pre durer, pre a rukk, an' odoi she lastered a chillico's nest. But the kanengro prastered alay the choomber, longodurus adree the tem.

   Wafri bak kairs   A choro mush ta jal alay,   But it mukks a boro mush   To chiv his kokero apre. {213}

TRANSLATION.

Once the cat went to see her cousin the hare. And there came a hunter, and the cat scrambled up the hill, further up, up a tree, and there she found a bird's nest. But the hare ran down the hill, far down into the country.

Bad luck sends a poor man further down, but it causes a great man to rise still more.

GUDLO XII. OF THE GIPSY WOMAN AND THE CHILD.

Pre yeck chairus a chi jalled adree a waver tem, an' she rikkered a gunno pre laki dumo with a baulo adree. A rakli who was ladge of her tikno chored the baulo avree the gunno and chivved the chavi adree. Pasch a waver hora the chi shooned the tikno rov (ruvving), and dicked adree the gunno in boro toob, and penned, "If the baulos in akovo tem puraben into chavos, sa do the chavos puraben adree?"

TRANSLATION.

Once a woman went into a strange land, and she carried a bag on her back with a pig in it. A girl who was ashamed of her child stole the pig from the bag and put the baby in (its place). After an hour the woman heard the child cry, and looked into the bag with great amazement, and said, "If the pigs in this country change into children, into what do the children change?"

GUDLO XIII. OF THE GIRL THAT WAS TO MARRY THE DEVIL.

'Pre yeck divvus a Rommany dye dukkered a rakli, and pookered laki that a kaulo rye kaumed her. But when the chi putchered her wongur, the rakli penned, "Puri dye, I haven't got a poshero to del tute. But pen mandy the nav of the kaulo rye." Then the dye shelled avree, very hunnalo, "Beng is the nav of tute's pirryno, and yuv se kaulo adusta."

If you chore puri juvas tute'll lel the beng.

TRANSLATION.

On a day a Gipsy mother told a girl's fortune, and said to her that a dark (black) gentleman loved her. But when the woman demanded her money, the girl said, "Old mother, I haven't got a halfpenny to give you. But tell me the name of the dark gentleman." Then the mother roared out, very angry, "Devil is the name of your sweetheart, and he is black enough."

If you cheat old women you will catch the devil.

GUDLO XIV. OF THE GIPSY WHO STOLE THE HORSE.

Yeckorus a mush chored a gry and jalled him avree adree a waver tem, and the gry and the mush jalled kushti bak kettenus. Penned the gry to his mush, "I kaums your covvas to wearus kushtier than mandy's, for there's kek chucknee or mellicus (pusimigree) adree them." "Kek," penned the mush pauli; "the trash I lel when mandy jins of the prastramengro an' the bitcherin' mush (krallis mush) is wafrier than any chucknee or busaha, an' they'd kair mandy to praster my miramon (mira-ben) avree any divvus."

TRANSLATION.

Once a man stole a horse and ran him away into another country, and the horse and the man became very intimate. Said the horse to the man, "I like your things to wear better than I do mine, for there's no whip or spur among them." "No," replied the man; "the fear I have when I think of the policeman and of the judge (sending or "transporting" man, or king's man) is worse than any whip or spur, and they would make me run my life away any day."

GUDLO XV. THE HALF-BLOOD GIPSY, HIS WIFE, AND THE PIG.

'Pre yeck divvus there was a mush a-piin' ma his Rommany chals adree a kitchema, an' pauli a chairus he got pash matto. An' he penned about mullo baulors, that *he* never hawed kek. Kenna-sig his juvo welled adree an' putched him to jal kerri, but yuv pookered her, "Kek--I won't jal kenna." Then she penned, "Well alang, the chavvis got kek habben." So she putchered him ajaw an' ajaw, an' he always rakkered her pauli "Kek." So she lelled a mullo baulor ap her dumo and wussered it 'pre the haumescro pre saw the foki, an' penned, "Lel the mullo baulor an' rummer it, an' mandy'll dick pauli the chavos."

TRANSLATION.

Once there was a man drinking with his Gipsy fellows in an alehouse, and after a while he got half drunk. And he said of pigs that had died a natural death, *he* never ate any. By-and-by his wife came in and asked him to go home, but he told her, "No--I won't go now." Then she said, "Come along, the children have no food." So she entreated him again and again, and he always answered "No." So she took a pig that had died a natural death, from her back and threw it on the table before all the people, and said, "Take the dead pig for a wife, and I will look after the children." {218}

GUDLO XVI. THE GIPSY TELLS THE STORY OF THE SEVEN WHISTLERS.

My raia, the gudlo of the Seven Whistlers, you jin, is adree the Scriptures--so they pookered mandy.

An' the Seven Whistlers (*Efta Shellengeri*) is seven spirits of ranis that jal by the ratti, 'pre the bavol, parl the heb, like chillicos. An' it pookers 'dree the Bible that the Seven Whistlers shell wherever they praster atut the bavol. But aduro timeus yeck jalled avree an' got nashered, and kenna there's only shove; but they pens 'em the Seven Whistlers. An' that sims the story tute pookered mandy of the Seven Stars.

TRANSLATION.

Sir, the story of the Seven Whistlers, you know, is in the Scriptures--so they told me.

An' the Seven Whistlers are seven spirits of ladies that go by the night, through the air, over the heaven, like birds. And it tells (us) in the Bible that the Seven Whistlers whistle wherever they fly across the air. But a long time ago one went away and got lost, and now there are only six; but they call them the Seven Whistlers. And that is like the story you told me of the Seven Stars. {219}

GUDLO XVII. AN OLD STORY WELL KNOWN TO ALL GIPSIES.

A Rommany rakli yeckorus jalled to a ker a-dukkerin'. A'ter she jalled avree, the rakli of the ker missered a plachta, and pookered the rye that the Rommany chi had chored it. So the rye jalled aduro pauli the tem, and latched the Rommany chals, and bitchered them to staruben. Now this was adree the puro chairus when they used to nasher mushis for any bitti covvo. And some of the Rommany chals were nashered, an' some pannied. An' sar the gunnos, an' kavis, and covvas of the Rommanis were chivved and pordered kettenus 'pre the bor adree the cangry-puv, an' kek mush tooled 'em. An' trin dood (or munti) pauli, the rakli was kairin' the baulors' habben at the kokero ker, when she latched the plachta they nashered trin dood adovo divvus. So the rakli jalled with the plachta ta laki rye, and penned, "Dick what I kaired on those chuvvenny, chori Rommany chals that were nashered and pannied for adovo bitti covvo adoi!"

And when they jalled to dick at the Rommanis' covvas pauli the bor adree the cangry-puv, the gunnos were pordo and chivved adree, chingered saw to cut-engroes, and they latched 'em full o' ruppeny covvos--rooys an' churls of sonnakai, an' oras, curros an' piimangris, that had longed o' the Rommany chals that were nashered an' bitchered padel.

TRANSLATION.

A Gipsy girl once went to a house to tell fortunes. After she went away, the girl of the house missed a pudding-bag (literally, *linen cloth*), and told the master the Gipsy girl had stolen it. So the master went far about the country, and found the Gipsies, and sent them to prison. Now this was in the old time when they used to hang people for any little thing. And some of the Gipsies were hung, and some transported (literally, *watered*). And all the bags, and kettles, and things of the Gipsies were thrown and piled together behind the hedge in the churchyard, and no man touched them. And three months after, the maid was preparing the pigs' food at the same house, when she found the linen cloth they lost three months (before) that day. So the girl went with the cloth to her master, and said, "See what I did to those poor, poor Gipsies that were hung and transported for that trifle (there)!"

And when they went to look at the Gipsies' things behind the hedge in the churchyard, the bags were full and burst, torn all to rags, and they found them full of silver things--spoons and knives of gold, and watches, cups and teapots, that had belonged to the Gipsies that were hung and transported. {221a}

GUDLO XVIII. HOW THE GIPSY WENT TO CHURCH.

Did mandy ever jal to kangry? Avali, dui koppas, and beshed a lay odoi. I was adree the tale tem o' sar, an' a rye putched mandy to well to kangry, an' I welled. And sar the ryas an' ranis dicked at mandy as I jalled adree. {221b} So I beshed puk-kenus mongin some geeros and dicked upar again the chumure praller my sherro, and there was a deer and a kanengro odoi chinned in the bar, an' kaired kushto. I shooned the rashai a-rakkerin'; and when the shunaben was kerro, I welled avree and jalled alay the drum to the kitchema.

I latchered the raias mush adree the kitchema; so we got matto odoi, an' were jallin' kerri alay the drum when we dicked the raias wardo a-wellin'. So we jalled sig 'dusta parl the bor, an' gavered our kokeros odoi adree the puv till the rye had jessed avree.

I dicked adovo rye dree the sala, and he putched mandy what I'd kaired the cauliko, pash kangry. I pookered him I'd pii'd dui or trin curros levinor and was pash matto. An' he penned mandy, "My mush was matto sar tute, and I nashered him." I pookered him ajaw, "I hope not, rya, for such a bitti covvo as dovo; an' he aint cammoben to piin' levinor, he's only used to pabengro, that don't kair him matto." But kek, the choro mush had to jal avree. An' that's sar I can rakker tute about my jallin' to kangry.

TRANSLATION.

Did I ever go to church? Yes, twice, and sat down there. I was in the lower land of all (Cornwall), and a gentleman asked me to go to church, and I went. And all the ladies and gentlemen looked at me as I went in. So I sat quietly among some men and looked up on the wall above my head, and there were a deer and a rabbit cut in the stone, beautifully done. I heard the clergyman speaking; and when the sermon was ended (literally, made), I came out and went down the road to the alehouse.

I found the gentleman's servant in the alehouse; so we got drunk there, and were going home down the road when we saw the gentleman's carriage coming. So we went quickly enough over the hedge, and hid ourselves there in the field until the gentleman was gone.

I saw the gentleman in the morning, and he asked me what I had done the day before, after church. I told him I'd drunk two or three cups of ale and was half tipsy. And he said, "My man was drunk as you, and I sent him off." I told him then, "I hope not, sir, for such a little thing as that; and he is not used to drink ale, he's only accustomed to cider, that don't intoxicate him." But no, the poor man had to go away. *And that's all I can tell you about my going to church*.

GUDLO XIX. WHAT THE LITTLE GIPSY GIRL TOLD HER BROTHER.

Penned the tikni Rommani chavi laki pal, "More mor the pishom, 'cause she's a Rommani, and kairs her jivaben jallin' parl the tem dukkerin' the ruzhas and lellin' the gudlo avree 'em, sar moro dye dukkers the ranis. An' ma wusser bars at the rookas, 'cause they're kaulos, an' kaulo ratt is Rommany ratt. An' maun pogger the bawris, for yuv rikkers his tan pre the dumo, sar moro puro dadas, an' so yuv's Rommany."

TRANSLATION.

Said the little Gipsy girl to her brother, "Don't kill the bee, because she is a Gipsy, and makes her living going about the country telling fortunes to the flowers and taking honey out of them, as our mother tells fortunes to the ladies. And don't throw stones at the rooks, because they are dark, and dark blood is Gipsy blood. And don't crush the snail, for he carries his tent on his back, like our old father" (*i.e.*, carries his home about, and so he too is Rommany).

GUDLO XX. HOW CHARLEY LEE PLAYED AT PITCH-AND-TOSS.

I jinned a tano mush yeckorus that nashered sar his wongur 'dree the toss-ring. Then he jalled kerri to his dadas' kanyas and lelled pange bar avree. Paul' a bitti chairus he dicked his dadas an' pookered lester he'd lelled pange bar avree his gunnas. But yuv's dadas penned, "Jal an, kair it ajaw and win some wongur againus!" So he jalled apopli to the toss-ring an' lelled sar his wongur pauli, an' pange bar ferridearer. So he jalled ajaw kerri to the tan, an' dicked his dadas beshtin' alay by the rikk o' the tan, and his dadas penned, "Sa did you keravit, my chavo?" "Kushto, dadas. I lelled sar my wongur pauli; and here's tute's wongur acai, an' a bar for tute an' shtar bar for mi-kokero."

An' that's tacho as ever you tool that pen in tute's waster--an' dovo mush was poor Charley Lee, that's mullo kenna.

TRANSLATION.

I knew a little fellow once that lost all his money in the toss-ring (*i.e*., at pitch-and-toss). Then he went home to his father's sacks and took five pounds out. After a little while he saw his father and told him he'd taken five pounds from his bags. But his father said, "Go on, spend it and win some more money!" So he went again to the toss-ring and got all his money back, and five pounds more. And going home, he saw his father sitting by the side of the tent, and his father said, "How did you succeed (*i.e*., *do it*), my son?" "Very well, father. I got all *my* money back; and here's *your* money now, and a pound for you and four pounds for myself."

And that's true as ever you hold that pen in your hand--and that man was poor Charley Lee, that's dead now.

GUDLO XXI. OF THE TINKER AND THE KETTLE.

A petulamengro hatched yeck divvus at a givescro ker, where the rani del him mass an' tood. While he was hawin' he dicked a kekavi sar chicklo an' bongo, pashall a boro hev adree, an' he putchered, "Del it a mandy an' I'll lel it avree for chichi, 'cause you've been so kushto an' kammoben to mandy." So she del it a lester, an' he jalled avree for trin cooricus, an' he keravit apre, an' kaired it pauno sar rupp. Adovo he welled akovo drum pauli, an' jessed to the same ker, an' penned, "Dick acai at covi kushti kekavi! I del shove trin mushis for it, an' tu shall lel it for the same wongur, 'cause you've been so kushto a mandy."

Dovo mush was like boot 'dusta mushis--wery cammoben to his kokero.

TRANSLATION.

A tinker stopped one day at a farmer's house, where the lady gave him meat and milk. While he was eating he saw a kettle all rusty and bent, with a great hole in it, and he asked, "Give it to me and I will take it away for nothing, because you have been so kind and obliging to me." So she gave it to him, and he went away for three weeks, and he repaired it (the kettle), and made it as bright (white) as silver. Then he went that road again, to the same house, and said, "Look here at this fine kettle! I gave six shillings for it, and you shall have it for the same money, because you have been so good to me."

That man was like a great many men--very benevolent to himself.

GUDLO XXII. THE STORY OF "ROMMANY JOTER."

If a Rommany chal gets nashered an' can't latch his drum i' the ratti, he shells avree, "*Hup*, *hup* -- *Rom-ma-ny*, *Rom-ma-ny jo-ter*!" When the chavvis can't latch the tan, it's the same gudlo, "*Rom-ma-ny jo-ter*!" Joter pens kett'nus.

And yeck ratti my dadas, sixty besh kenna, was pirryin' par the weshes to tan, an' he shooned a bitti gudlo like bitti ranis a rakkerin' puro tacho Rommanis, and so he jalled from yeck boro rukk to the waver, and paul' a cheirus he dicked a tani rani, and she was shellin' avree for her miraben, "*Rom-ma-ny*, *Rom-ma-ny jo-ter*!" So my dada shokkered ajaw, "*Rom-ma-ny chal*, *ak-ai*!" But as he shelled there welled a boro bavol, and the bitti ranis an' sar prastered avree i' the heb like chillicos adree a starmus, and all he shunned was a savvaben and "Rom-ma- ny jo-ter!" shukaridir an' shukaridir, pash sar was kerro.

An' you can dick by dovo that the kukalos, an' fairies, an' mullos, and chovi-hans all rakker puro tacho Rommanis, 'cause that's the old 'Gyptian jib that was penned adree the Scripture tem.

TRANSLATION.

If a Gipsy is lost and cannot find his way in the night, he cries out, "Hup, hup-- Rom-ma-ny, Rom-ma-ny jo-ter!" When the children cannot find the tent, it is the same cry, "*Rom-ma-ny jo-ter*!" Joter means together.

And one night my father, sixty years ago (literally, *now*), was walking through the woods to his tent, and he heard a little cry like little ladies talking real old Gipsy, and so he went from one great tree to the other (*i.e*., concealing himself), and after a while he saw a little lady, and she was crying out as if for her life, "*Rom-ma-ny*, *Rom-ma-ny jo-ter*!" So my father cried again, "*Gipsy*, *here*!" But as he hal-looed there came a great blast of wind, and the little ladies and all flew away in the sky like birds in a storm, and all he heard was a laughing and "*Rom-ma-ny jo-ter*!" softer and softer, till all was done.

And you can see by that that the goblins (dwarfs, mannikins), and fairies, and ghosts, and witches, and all talk real old Gipsy, because that is the old Egyptian language that was talked in the Scripture land.

GUDLO XXIII. OF THE RICH GIPSY AND THE PHEASANT.

Yeckorus a Rommany chal kaired adusta wongur, and was boot barvelo an' a boro rye. His chuckko was kashno, an' the crafnies 'pre lester chuckko were o' son-nakai, and his graias solivaris an' guiders were sar ruppeny. Yeck divvus this here Rommany rye was hawin' habben anerjal the krallis's chavo, an' they hatched adree a weshni kanni that was kannelo, but saw the mushis penned it was kushtidearer. "Bless mi-Duvel!" rakkered the Rommany rye shukar to his juvo, "tu and mandy have hawed mullo mass boot 'dusta cheiruses, mi-deari, but never soomed kek so wafro as dovo. It kauns worse than a mullo grai!"

Boro mushis an' bitti mushis sometimes kaum covvas that waver mushis don't jin.

TRANSLATION.

Once a Gipsy made much money, and was very rich and a great gentleman. His coat was silk, and the buttons on his coat were of gold, and his horse's bridle and reins were all silver. One day this Gipsy gentleman was eating (at table) opposite to the king's son, and they brought in a pheasant that smelt badly, but all the people said it was excellent. "Bless me, God!" said the Gipsy gentleman softly (whispering) to his wife, "you and I have eaten dead meat (meat that died a natural death) many a time, my dear, but never smelt anything so bad as that. It stinks worse than a dead horse!"

Great men and small men sometimes like (agree in liking things) that which other people do not understand.

GUDLO XXIV. THE GIPSY AND THE "VISITING-CARDS."

Yeckorus a choro Rommany chal dicked a rani hatch taller the wuder of a boro ker an' mukked adovo a bitti lil. Then he putched the rakli, when the rani jessed avree, what the lil kaired. Adoi the rakli pukkered lesco it was for her rani ta jin kun'd welled a dick her. "Avali!" penned the Rommany chal; "*that's* the way the Gorgios mukks their patteran! *We* mukks char apre the drum."

The grai mukks his pirro apre the drum, an' the sap kairs his trail adree the puv.

TRANSLATION.

Once a poor Gipsy saw a lady stop before the door of a great house and left there a card (little letter). Then he asked the girl, when the lady went away, what the card meant (literally, *did*). Then (there) the girl told him it was for her lady to know who had come to see her. "Yes!" said the Gipsy; "so that is the way the Gorgios leave their sign! *We* leave grass on the road."

The horse leaves his track on the road, and the snake makes his trail in the dust.

GUDLO XXV. THE GIPSY IN THE FOREST.

When I was beshin' alay adree the wesh tale the bori rukkas, mandy putched a tikno chillico to latch mandy a bitti moro, but it jalled avree an' I never dicked it kekoomi. Adoi I putched a boro chillico to latch mandy a curro o' tatti panni, but it jalled avree paul' the waver. Mandy never putchered the rukk parl my sherro for kek, but when the bavol welled it wussered a lay to mandy a hundred ripe kori.

TRANSLATION.

When I was sitting down in the forest under the great trees, I asked a little bird to bring (find) me a little bread, but it went away and I never saw it again. Then I asked a great bird to bring me a cup of brandy, but it flew away after the other. I never asked the tree over my head for anything, but when the wind came it threw down to me a hundred ripe nuts.

GUDLO XXVI. THE GIPSY FIDDLER AND THE YOUNG LADY.

Yeckorus a tano mush was kellin' kushto pre the boshomengro, an' a kushti dickin rani pookered him, "Tute's killaben is as sano as best-tood." And he rakkered ajaw, "Tute's mui's gudlo sar pishom, an' I'd cammoben to puraben mi tood for tute's pishom."

Kushto pash kushto kairs ferridearer.

TRANSLATION.

Once a young man was playing well upon the violin, and a beautiful lady told him, "Your playing is as soft as cream." And he answered, "Your mouth (*i.e.*, lips or words) is sweet as honey, and I would like to exchange my cream for your honey."

Good with good makes better.

GUDLO XXVII. HOW THE GIPSY DANCED A HOLE THROUGH A STONE.

Yeckorus some plochto Rommany chals an' juvas were kellin' the pash-divvus by dood tall' a boro ker, and yeck penned the waver, "I'd be cammoben if dovo ker was mandy's." And the rye o' the ker, kun sus dickin' the kellaben, rakkered,

"When tute kells a hev muscro the bar you're hatchin' apre, mandy'll del tute the ker." Adoi the Rom tarried the bar apre, an' dicked it was hollow tale, and sar a curro 'pre the waver rikk. So he lelled dui sastern chokkas and kelled sar the ratti 'pre the bar, kairin' such a gudlo you could shoon him a mee avree; an' adree the sala he had kaired a hev adree the bar as boro as lesters sherro. So the barvelo rye del him the fino ker, and sar the mushis got matto, hallauter kettenus.

Many a cheirus I've shooned my puri dye pen that a bar with a hev adree it kairs kammoben.

TRANSLATION.

Once some jolly Gipsy men and girls were dancing in the evening by moonlight before a great house, and one said to the other, "I'd be glad if that house was mine." And the gentleman of the house, who was looking at the dancing, said, "When you dance a hole through (in the centre of) the stone you are standing on, I'll give you the house." Then the Gipsy pulled the stone up, and saw it was hollow underneath, and like a cup on the other side. So he took two iron shoes and danced all night on the stone, making such a noise you could hear him a mile off; and in the morning he had made a hole in the stone as large as his head. So the rich gentleman gave him the fine house, and all the people got drunk, all together.

Many a time I've heard my old mother say that a stone with a hole in it brings luck.

GUDLO XXVIII. STORY OF THE GENTLEMAN AND THE GIPSY.

Yeckorus a boro rye wouldn't mukk a choro, pauvero, chovveny Rommany chal hatch odoi 'pre his farm. So the Rommany chal jalled on a puv apre the waver rikk o' the drum, anerjal the ryas beshaben. And dovo ratti the ryas ker pelled alay; kek kash of it hatched apre, only the foki that loddered adoi hullered their kokeros avree ma their miraben. And the ryas tikno chavo would a-mullered if a Rommany juva had not lelled it avree their pauveri bitti tan.

An' dovo's sar *tacho like my dad*, an' to the divvus kenna they pens that puv the Rommany Puv.

TRANSLATION.

Once a great gentleman would not let a poor, poor, poor Gipsy stay on his farm. So the Gipsy went to a field on the other side of the way, opposite the gentleman's residence. And that night the gentleman's house fell down; not a stick of it remained standing, only the people who lodged there carried themselves out (*i.e* ., escaped) with their lives. And the gentleman's little babe would have died if a Gipsy woman had not taken it into their poor little tent.

And that's all **true as my father**, and to this day they call that field the Gipsy Field.

GUDLO XXIX. HOW THE GIPSY WENT INTO THE WATER.

Yeck divvus a prastramengro prastered pauli a Rommany chal, an' the chal jalled adree the panni, that was pordo o' boro bittis o' floatin' shill, and there he hatched pall his men with only his sherro avree. "Hav avree," shelled a rye that was wafro in his see for the pooro rnush, "an' we'll mukk you jal!" "Kek," penned the Rom; "I shan't jal." "Well avree," penned the rye ajaw, "an' I'll del tute pange bar!" "**Kek**," rakkered the Rom. "Jal avree," shokkered the rye, "an' I'll del tute pange bar an' a nevvi chukko!" "Will you del mandy a walin o' tatto panni too?" putched the Rommany chal. "Avail, avail," penned the rye; "but for Duveleste hav' avree the panni!" "Kushto," penned the Rommany chal, "for cammoben to tute, rya, I'll jal avree!" {235}

TRANSLATION.

Once a policeman chased a Gipsy, and the Gipsy ran into the river, that was full of great pieces of floating ice, and there he stood up to his neck with only his head out. "Come out," cried a gentleman that pitied the poor man, "and we'll let you go!" "No," said the Gipsy; "I won't move." "Come out," said the gentleman again, "and I'll give you five pounds!" "No," said the Gipsy. "Come out," cried the gentleman, "and I'll give you five pounds and a new coat!" "Will you give me a glass of brandy too?" asked the Gipsy. "Yes, yes," said the gentleman; "but for God's sake come out of the water!" "Well," exclaimed the Gipsy, "to oblige you, sir, I'll come out!"

GUDLO XXX. THE GIPSY AND HIS TWO MASTERS.

"Savo's tute's rye?" putched a ryas mush of a Rommany chal. "I've dui ryas," pooked the Rommany chal: "Duvel's the yeck an' beng's the waver. Mandy kairs booti for the beng till I've lelled my yeckora habben, an' pallers mi Duvel pauli ajaw."

TRANSLATION.

"Who is your master?" asked a gentleman's servant of a Gipsy. "I've two masters," said the Gipsy: "God is the one, and the devil is the other. I work for the devil till I have got my dinner (one-o'clock food), and after that follow the Lord."

GUDLO XXXI. THE LITTLE GIPSY BOY AT THE SILVERSMITH'S.

A bitti chavo jalled adree the boro gav pash his dadas, an' they hatched taller the hev of a ruppenomengro's buddika sar pordo o' kushti-dickin covvas. "O da-das," shelled the tikno chavo, "what a boro choromengro dovo mush must be to a' lelled so boot adusta rooys an' horas!"

A tacho covva often dicks sar a hokkeny (huckeny) covva; an dovo's sim of a tacho mush, but a juva often dicks tacho when she isn't.

TRANSLATION.

A little boy went to the great village (*i.e*., London) with his father, and they stopped before the window of a silversmith's shop all full of pretty things. "O fa-ther," cried the small boy, "what a great thief that man must be to have got so many spoons and watches!"

A true thing often looks like a false one; and the same is true (and that's *same*) of a true man, but a girl often looks right when she is not.

GUDLO XXXII. THE GIPSY'S DREAM.

Mandy sutto'd I was pirraben lang o' tute, an' I dicked mandy's pen odoi 'pre the choomber. Then I was pirryin' ajaw parl the puvius, an' I welled to the panni paul' the Beng's Choomber, an' adoi I dicked some ranis, saw nango barrin' a pauno plachta 'pre lengis sherros, adree the panni pash their bukkos. An' I pookered len-gis, "Mi-ranis, I putch tute's cammoben; I didn't jin tute sus acai." But yeck pre the wavers penned mandy boot kushti cammoben, "Chichi, mor dukker your-kokero; we just welled alay acai from the ker to lel a bitti bath." An' she savvy'd sa kushto, but they all jalled avree glan mandy sar the bavol, an' tute was hatchin' pash a maudy sar the cheirus.

So it pens, "when you dick ranis sar dovo, you'll muller kushto." Well, if it's to be akovo, I kaum it'll be a booti cheirus a-wellin.' Tacho!

TRANSLATION.

I dreamed I was walking with you, and I saw my sister (a fortune-teller) there upon the hill. Then I (found myself) walking again over the field, and I came to the water near the Devil's Dyke, and there I saw some ladies, quite naked excepting a white cloth on their heads, in the water to the waists. And I said to them, "Ladies, I beg your pardon; I did not know you were here." But one among the rest said to me very kindly, "No matter, don't trouble yourself; we just came down here from the house to take a little bath." And she smiled sweetly, but they all vanished before me like the cloud (wind), and you were standing by me all the time.

So it means, "***when you see ladies like that, you will die happily***." Well, if it's to be that, I hope it will be a long time coming. Yes, indeed.

GUDLO XXXIII. OF THE GIRL AND HER LOVER.

Yeckorus, boot hundred beshes the divvus acai, a juva was wellin' to chore a yora. "Mukk mandy hatch," penned the yora, "an' I'll sikker tute ki tute can lel a tikno pappni." So the juva lelled the tikno pappni, and it pookered laki, "Mukk mandy jal an' I'll sikker tute ki tute can chore a bori kani." Then she chored the bori kani, an' it shelled avree, "Mukk mandy jal an' I'll sikker tute ki you can loure a rani-chillico." And when she lelled the rani-chillico, it penned, "Mukk mandy jal an' I'll sikker tute odoi ki tute can lel a guruvni's tikno." So she lelled the guruvni's tikno, an' it shokkered and ruvved, an' rakkered, "Mukk mandy jal an' I'll sikker tute where to lel a fino grai." An' when she loured the grai, it penned laki, "Mukk mandy jal an' I'll rikker tute to a kushto-dick barvelo rye who kaums a pirreny." So she lelled the kushto tauno rye, an' she jivved with lester kushto yeck cooricus; but pash dovo he pookered her to jal avree, he didn't kaum her kekoomi. "Sa a wafro mush is tute," ruvved the rakli, "to bitcher mandy avree! For tute's cammoben I delled avree a yora, a tikno pappni, a boro kani, a rani-chillico, a guruvni's tikno, an' a fino grai." "Is dovo tacho?" putched the raklo. "'Pre my mullo dadas!' sovahalled the rakli," I del 'em sar apre for tute, yeck paul the waver, an' kenna tu bitchers mandy avree!" "So 'p mi-Duvel!" penned the rye, "if tute nashered sar booti covvas for mandy, I'll rummer tute." So they were rummobend.

Avali, there's huckeny (hokkeny) tachobens and tacho huckabens. You can sovahall pre the lil adovo.

TRANSLATION.

Once, many hundred years ago (to-day now), a girl was going to steal an egg. "Let me be," said the egg, "and I will show you where you can get a duck." So the girl got the duck, and it said (told) to her, "Let me go and I will show you where you can get a goose" (large hen). Then she stole the goose, and it cried out, "Let me go and I'll show you where you can steal a turkey" (lady-bird). And when she took the turkey, it said, "Let me go and I'll show you where you can get a calf." So she got the calf, and it bawled and wept, and cried, "Let me go and I'll show you where to get a fine horse." And when she stole the horse, it said to her, "Let me go and I'll carry you to a handsome, rich gentleman who wants a sweetheart." So she got the nice young gentleman, and lived with him pleasantly one week; but then he told her to go away, he did not want her any more. "What a bad man you are," wept the girl, "to send me away! For your sake I gave away an egg, a duck, a goose, a turkey, a calf, and a fine horse." "Is that true?" asked the youth. "By my dead father!" swore the girl, "I gave them all up for you, one after the other, and now you send me away!" "So help me God!" said the gentleman, "if you lost so many things for me, I'll marry you." So they were married.

Yes, there are false truths and true lies. You may kiss the book on *that*.

GUDLO XXXIV. THE GIPSY TELLS OF WILL-O'-THE-WISP.

Does mandy jin the lav adree Rommanis for a Jack-o'-lantern--the dood that prasters, and hatches, an' kells o' the ratti, parl the panni, adree the puvs? *Avali*; some pens 'em the Momeli Mullos, and some the Bitti Mullos. They're bitti gee-ros who rikker tute adree the gogemars, an' sikker tute a dood till you're all jalled apre a wafro drum an nashered, an' odoi they chiv their kokeros pauli an' savs at tute. Mandy's dicked their doods adusta cheiruses, an' kekoomi; but my pal dicked langis muis pash mungwe yeck ratti. He was jallin' langus an' dicked their doods, and jinned it was the yag of lesters tan. So he pallered 'em, an' they tadered him dukker the drum, parl the bors, weshes, puvius, gogemars, till they lelled him adree the panni, an then savvy'd avree. And odoi he dicked lender pre the waver rikk, ma lesters kokerus yakkis, an' they were bitti mushis, bitti chovihanis, about dui peeras boro. An' my pal was bengis hunnalo, an' sovahalled pal' lengis, "If I lelled you acai, you ratfolly juckos! if I nashered you, I'd chin tutes curros!" An' he jalled to tan ajaw an' pookered mandy saw dovo 'pre dovo rat. "Kun sus adovo?" Avali, rya; dovo was pash Kaulo Panni--near Blackwater.

TRANSLATION.

Do I know the word in Rommanis for a Jack-o'-lantern--the light that runs, and stops, and dances by night, over the water, in the fields? Yes; some call them the Light Ghosts, and some the Little Ghosts. They're little men who lead you into the waste and swampy places, and show you a light until you have gone astray and are lost, and then they turn themselves around and laugh at you. I have seen their lights many a time, and nothing more; but my brother saw their faces close and opposite to him (directly ***vis-a-vis***) one night. He was going along and saw their lights, and thought it was the fire of his tent. So he followed them, and they drew him from the road over hedges, woods, fields, and lonely marshes till they got him in the water, and then laughed out loud. And there he saw them with his own eyes, on the opposite side, and they were little fellows, little goblins, about two feet high. And my brother was devilish angry, and swore at them! "If I had you here, you wretched dogs! if I caught you, I'd cut your throats!" And he went home and told me all that that night. " ***Where was it***?" Yes, sir; that was near Blackwater.

GUDLO XXXV. THE GIPSY EXPLAINS WHY THE FLOUNDER HAS HIS MOUTH ON ONE SIDE.

Yeckorus sar the matchis jalled an' suvved kettenescrus 'dree the panni. And yeck penned as yuv was a boro mush, an' the waver rakkered ajaw sa yuv was a borodiro mush, and sar pookered sigan ket'nus how lengis were borodirer mushis. Adoi the flounder shelled avree for his meriben "Mandy's the krallis of you sar!" an' he shelled so surrelo he kaired his mui bongo, all o' yeck rikkorus. So to akovo divvus acai he's penned the Krallis o' the Matchis, and rikkers his mui bongo sar o' yeck sidus.

Mushis shouldn't shell too shunaben apre lengis kokeros.

TRANSLATION.

Once all the fish came and swam together in the water. And one said that he was a great person, and the other declared that he was a greater person, and (at last) all cried out at once what great characters (men) they all were. Then the flounder shouted for his life, "I'm the king of you all!" and he roared so violently he twisted his mouth all to one side. So to this day he is called the King of the Fishes, and bears his face crooked all on one side.

Men should not boast too loudly of themselves.

GUDLO XXXVI. A GIPSY ACCOUNT OF THE TRUE ORIGIN OF THE FISH CALLED OLD MAIDS OR YOUNG MAIDS.

Yeckorus kushti-dickin raklos were suvvin' 'dree the lun panni, and there welled odoi some plochti raklis an' juvas who pooked the tano ryas to hav' avree an' choomer 'em. But the raklos wouldn't well avree, so the ranis rikkered their rivabens avree an' pirried adree the panni paul' lendy. An' the ryas who were kandered alay, suvved andurer 'dree the panni, an' the ranis pallered 'em far avree till they were saw latchered, raklos and raklis. So the tauno ryas were purabened into Barini Mushi Matchis because they were too ladge (latcho) of the ranis that kaumed 'em, and the ranis were kaired adree Puri Rani Matchis and Tani Rani Matchis because they were too tatti an' ruzli.

Raklos shouldn't be too ladge, nor raklis be too boro of their kokeros.

TRANSLATION.

Once some handsome youths were swimming in the sea, and there came some wanton women and girls who told the young men to come out and kiss them. But the youths would not come out, so the ladies stripped themselves and ran into the water after them. And the gentles who were driven away swam further into the water, and the ladies followed them far away till all were lost, boys and girls. So the young men were changed into Codfish because they were too shy of the girls that loved them, and the ladies were turned into Old Maids and Young Maids because they were too wanton and bold.

Men should not be too modest, nor girls too forward.

GUDLO XXXVII. HOW LORD COVENTRY LEAPED THE GIPSY TENT. A TRUE STORY.

I dicked Lord Coventry at the Worcester races. He kistured lester noko grai adree the steeple-chase for the ruppeny--kek,--a sonnakai tank I think it was,--but he nashered. It was dovo tano rye that yeck divvus in his noko park dicked a Rommany chal's tan pash the rikk of a bor; and at yeck leap he kistered apre the bor, and jalled right atut an' parl the Rommany chal's tan. "Ha, kun's acai?" he shelled, as he dicked the tikno kaulos; "a Rommany chal's tan!" And from dovo divvus he mukked akovo Rom hatch his cammoben 'pre his puv. Tacho.

Ruzlo mushis has boro sees.

TRANSLATION.

I saw Lord Coventry at the Worcester races. He rode his own horse in the steeple-chase for the silver--no, it was a gold tankard, I think, but he lost.

It was that young gentleman who one day in his own park saw a Gipsy tent by the side of a hedge, and took a flying leap over tent, hedge, and all. "Ha, what's here?" he cried, as he saw the little brown children; "a Gipsy's tent!" And from that day he let that Gipsy stay as much as he pleased on his land.

Bold men have generous hearts.

GUDLO XXXVIII. OF MR BARTLETT'S LEAP.

Dovo's sim to what they pens of Mr Bartlett in Glo'stershire, who had a fino tem pash Glo'ster an' Bristol, where he jivved adree a boro ker. Kek mush never dicked so booti weshni juckalos or weshni kannis as yuv rikkered odoi. They prastered atut saw the drumyas sim as kanyas. Yeck divvus he was kisterin' on a kushto grai, an' he dicked a Rommany chal rikkerin' a truss of gib-puss 'pre lester dumo pral a bitti drum, an' kistered 'pre the pooro mush, puss an' sar. I jins that puro mush better 'n I jins tute, for I was a'ter yeck o' his raklis yeckorus; he had kushti-dick raklis, an' he was old Knight Locke. "Puro," pens the rye, "did I kair you trash?" "I mang tute's shunaben, rya," pens Locke pauli; "I didn't jin tute sus wellin'!" So puro Locke hatched odoi 'pre dovo tem sar his miraben, an' that was a kushti covva for the puro Locke.

TRANSLATION.

That is like what is told of Mr Bartlett in Gloucestershire, who had a fine place near Gloucester and Bristol, where he lived in a great house. No man ever saw so many foxes or pheasants as he kept there. They ran across all the paths like hens. One day he was riding on a fine horse, when he saw a Gipsy carrying a truss of wheat-straw on his back up a little path, and leaped over the poor man, straw and all. I knew that old man better than I know you, for I was after one of his daughters then; he had beautiful girls, and he was old Knight Locke. "Old fellow," said the gentleman, "did I frighten you?" "I beg your pardon, sir," said Locke after him; "I didn't know you were coming!" So old Locke stayed on that land all his life, and that was a good thing for old Locke.

GUDLO XXXIX. THE GIPSY, THE PIG, AND THE MUSTARD.

Yeckorus a Rommany chal jalled to a boro givescroker sa's the rye sus hawin'. And sikk's the Rom wan't a-dickin', the rye all-sido pordered a kell-mallico pash kris, an' del it to the Rommany chal. An' sa's the kris dantered adree his gullo, he was pash tassered, an' the panni welled in his yakkas. Putched the rye, "Kun's tute ruvvin' ajaw for?" An' he rakkered pauli, "The kris lelled mandys bavol ajaw." Penned the rye, "I kaum the kris'll del tute kushti bak." "Parraco, rya," penned the Rom pauli; "I'll kommer it kairs dovo." Sikk's the rye bitchered his sherro, the Rommany chal loured the krissko-curro ma the ruppeny rooy, an' kek dicked it.

The waver divvus anpauli, dovo Rom jalled to the ryas baulo- tan, an' dicked odoi a boro rikkeno baulo, an' gillied, "I'll dick acai if I can kair tute ruv a bitti."

Now, rya, you must jin if you del a baulor kris adree a pabo, he can't shell avree or kair a gudlo for his miraben, an' you can rikker him bissin', or chiv him apre a wardo, an' jal andurer an' kek jin it. An' dovo's what the Rommany chal kaired to the baulor, pash the sim kris; an' as he bissered it avree an' pakkered it adree a gun-no, he penned shukkar adree the baulor's kan, "Calico tute's rye hatched my bavol, an' the divvus I've hatched tute's; an' yeckorus your rye kaumed the kris would del mandy kushti bak, and kenna it *has* del mengy kushtier bak than ever he jinned."

Ryes must be sig not to kair pyass an' trickis atop o' choro mushis.

TRANSLATION.

Once a Gipsy went to a great farmhouse as the gentleman sat at table eating. And so soon as the Gipsy looked away, the gentleman very quietly filled a cheese-cake with mustard and gave it to the Gipsy. When the mustard bit in his throat, he was half choked, and the tears came into his eyes. The gentleman asked him, "What are you weeping for now?" And he replied, "The mustard took my breath away." The gentleman said, "I hope the mustard will give you good luck!" "Thank you, sir," answered the Gipsy; "I'll take care it does" (that). As soon as the gentleman turned his head, the Gipsy stole the mustard-pot with the silver spoon, and no one saw it. The next day after, that Gipsy went to the gentleman's pig-pen, and saw there a great fine-looking pig, and sang, "I'll see now if I can make *you* weep a bit."

Now, sir, you must know that if you give a pig mustard in an apple, he can't cry out or squeal for his life, and you can carry him away, or throw him on a wag-gon, and get away, and nobody will know it. And that is what the Gipsy did to the pig, with the same mustard; and as he ran it away and put it in a bag, he whispered softly into the pig's ear, "Yesterday your master stopped my breath, and to-day I've stopped yours; and once your master hoped the mustard would give me good luck, and now it *has* given me better luck than he ever imagined."

Gentlemen must be careful not to make sport of and play tricks on poor men.

GUDLO XL. EXPLAINING THE ORIGIN OF A CURRENT GIPSY PROVERB OR SAYING.

Trin or shtor beshes pauli kenna yeck o' the Petulengros dicked a boro mullo baulor adree a bitti drum. An' sig as he latched it, some Rommany chals welled alay an' dicked this here Rommany chal. So Petulengro he shelled avree, "A fino baulor! saw tulloben! jal an the sala an' you shall have pash." And they welled apopli adree the sala and lelled pash sar tacho. And ever sense dovo divvus it's a rakkerben o' the Rommany chals, "Sar tulloben; jal an the sala an' tute shall lel your pash."

TRANSLATION.

Three or four years ago one of the Smiths found a great dead pig in a lane. And just as he found it, some Gipsies came by and saw this Rommany. So Smith bawled out to them, "A fine pig! all fat! come in the morning and you shall have half." And they returned in the morning and got half, all right. And ever since it has been a saying with the Gipsies, "It's **all fat**; come in the morning and get your half."

GUDLO XLI. THE GIPSY'S FISH-HOOK.

Yeckorus a rye pookered a Rommany chal he might jal matchyin' 'dree his panni, and he'd del lester the cammoben for trin mushi, if he'd only matchy with a bongo sivv an' a punsy-ran. So the Rom jalled with India- drab kaired apre moro, an' he drabbered saw the matchas adree the panni, and rikkered avree his wardo sar pordo. A boro cheirus pauli dovo, the rye dicked the Rommany chal, an' penned, "You choramengro, did tute lel the matchas avree my panni with a hook?" "Ayali, rya, with a hook," penned the Rom pale, werry sido. "And what kind of a hook?" "Rya," rakkered the Rom, "it was yeck o' the longi kind, what we pens in amandis jib a hookaben" (*i.e*., huckaben or hoc'aben).

When you del a mush cammoben to lel matchyas avree tute's panni, you'd better hatch adoi an' dick how he kairs it.

TRANSLATION.

Once a gentleman told a Gipsy he might fish in his pond, and he would give him permission to do so for a shilling, but that he must only fish with a hook and a fishing-pole (literally, crooked needle). So the Gipsy went with India-drab (juice of the berries of **Indicus cocculus**) made up with bread, and poisoned all the fish in the pond, and carried away his waggonful. A long time after, the gentleman met the Gipsy, and said, "You thief, did you catch the fish in my pond with a hook?" "Yes, sir, with a hook," replied the Gipsy very quietly. "And what kind of a hook?" "Sir," said the Gipsy, "it was one of the long kind, what we call in our language a hookaben" (*i.e*., **a lie or trick**).

When you give a man leave to fish in your pond, you had better be present and see how he does it.

GUDLO XLII. THE GIPSY AND THE SNAKE.

If you more the first sappa you dicks, tute'll more the first enemy you've got. That's what 'em pens, but I don't jin if it's tacho or nettus. And yeckorus there was a werry wafro mush that was allers a-kairin' wafri covvabens. An' yeck divvus he dicked a sap in the wesh, an' he prastered paller it with a bori churi adree lester waster and chinned her sherro apre. An' then he rakkered to his kokerus, "Now that I've mored the sap, I'll lel the jivaben of my wenomest enemy." And just as he penned dovo lav he delled his pirro atut the danyas of a rukk, an' pet alay and chivved the churi adree his bukko. An' as he was beshin' alay a-mullerin' 'dree the weshes, he penned to his kokerus, "Avali, I dicks kenna that dovo's tacho what they pookers about morin' a sappa; for I never had kek worser ennemis than I've been to mandy's selfus, and what wells of morin' innocen hanimals is kek kushtoben."

TRANSLATION.

If you kill the first snake you see, you'll kill the first (principal) enemy you have. That is what they say, but I don't know whether it is true or not. And once there was a very bad man who was always doing bad deeds. And one day he saw a snake in the forest, and ran after it with a great knife in his hand and cut her head off. And then he said to himself, "Now that I've killed the snake, I'll take the life of my most vindictive (literally, most venomous) enemy." And just as he spoke that word he struck his foot against the roots of a tree, and fell down and drove the knife into his own body (liver or heart). And as he lay dying in the forests, he said to himself, "Yes, I see now that it is true what they told me as to killing a snake; for I never had any worse enemy than I have been to myself, and what comes of killing innocent animals is naught good."

GUDLO XLIII. THE STORY OF THE GIPSY AND THE BULL.

Yeckorus there was a Rommany chal who was a boro koorin' mush, a surrelo mush, a boro-wasteni mush, werry toonery an' hunnalo. An' he penned adusta cheiruses that kek geero an' kek covva 'pre the drumyas couldn't trasher him. But yeck divvus, as yuv was jallin' langs the drum with a waver pal, chunderin' an' hookerin' an' lunterin', an' shorin' his kokero how he could koor the puro bengis' selfus, they shooned a guro a-goorin' an' googerin', an' the first covva they jinned he prastered like divius at 'em, an' these here geeros prastered apre ye rukk, an' the boro koorin' mush that was so flick o' his wasters chury'd first o' saw (sar), an' hatched duri-dirus from the puv pre the limmers. An' he beshed adoi an' dicked ye bullus wusserin' an' chongerin' his trushnees sar aboutus, an' kellin' pre lesters covvas, an' poggerin' to cutengroes saw he lelled for lesters miraben. An' whenever the bavol pudered he was atrash he'd pelt-a-lay 'pre the shinger-ballos of the gooro (guro). An' so they beshed adoi till the sig of the sala, when the mush who dicked a'ter the gruvnis welled a-pirryin' by an' dicked these here chals beshin' like chilli-cos pre the rukk, an' patched lengis what they were kairin' dovo for. So they pook-ered him about the bullus, an' he hankered it avree; an' they welled alay an' jalled andurer to the kitchema, for there never was dui mushis in 'covo tem that kaumed a droppi levinor koomi than lender. But pale dovo divvus that trusheni mush never sookered he couldn't be a trashni mush no moreus. Tacho.

TRANSLATION.

Once there was a Gipsy who was a great fighting man, a strong man, a great boxer, very bold and fierce. And he said many a time that no man and no thing on the roads could frighten him. But one day, as he was going along the road with an-other man (his friend), exaggerating and bragging and boasting, and praising him-self that he could beat the old devil himself, they heard a bull bellowing and growl-ing, and the first thing they knew he ran like mad at them; and these men hurried up a tree, and the great fighting man that was so handy with his fists climbed first of all, and got (placed) himself furtherest from the ground on the limbs. And he sat there and saw the bull tossing and throwing his baskets all about, and dancing on his things, and breaking to pieces all he had for his living. And whenever the wind blew he was afraid he would fall on the horns of the bull. And so they sat there till daybreak, when the man who looked after the cows came walking by and saw these fellows sitting like birds on the tree, and asked them what they were doing that for. So they told him about the bull, and he drove it away; and they came down and went on to the alehouse, for there never were two men in this country that wanted a drop of beer more than they. But after that day that thirsty man never boasted he could not be a frightened man. True.

GUDLO XLIV. THE GIPSY AND HIS THREE SWEETHEARTS.

Yeckorus a tano mush kaired his cammoben ta trin juvas kett'nus an' kek o' the trin jinned yuv sus a pirryin' ye waver dui. An 'covo raklo jivved adree a bitti tan pash the rikkorus side o' the boro lun panni, an' yeck ratti sar the chais welled shikri kett'nus a lester, an' kek o' the geeris jinned the wavers san lullerin adoi. So they jalled sar-sigan kett'nus, an' rakkered, "Sarshan!" ta yeck chairus. An' dovo raklo didn't jin what juva kaumed lester ferridirus, or kun yuv kaumed ye ferridirus, so sar the shtor besht-a-lay sum, at the habbenescro, and yuv del len habben an' levinor. Yeck hawed booti, but ye waver dui wouldn't haw kek, yeck pii'd, but ye waver dui wouldn't pi chommany, 'cause they were sar hunnali, and sookeri an' kuried. So the raklo penned lengis, yuv sos atrash if yuv lelled a juva 'at couldn't haw, she wouldn't jiv, so he rummored the rakli that hawed her habben.

All'ers haw sar the habben foki banders apre a tute, an' tute'll jal sikker men dush an' tukli.

TRANSLATION.

Once a young man courted three girls together, and none of the three knew he was courting the two others. And that youth lived in a little place near the side of the great salt water, and one night all the girls came at once together to him, and none of the girls knew the others were coming there. So they went all quick together, and said "Good evening," (sarishan means really "How are you?") at the same time. And that youth did not know which girl liked him best, or whom he loved best; so all the four sat down together at the table, and he gave them food and beer. One ate plenty, but the other two would eat nothing; one drank, but the other two would not drink something, because they were all angry, and grieved, and worried. So the youth told them he was afraid if he took a wife that could not eat, she would not live, so he married the girl that ate her food.

Always eat all the food that people give you (literally share out to you), and you will go readily (securely) through sorrow and trouble.

GUDLO XLV. THE GIPSIES AND THE SMUGGLERS. A TRUE STORY.

Yeckorus, most a hundred besh kenna, when mi dadas sus a chavo, yeck ratti a booti Rommany chals san millerin kettenescrus pash the boro panni, kun sar-sig the graias ankaired a-wickerin an' ludderin an' nuckerin' an kairin a boro gudli, an' the Rommanis shuned a shellin, an' dicked mushis prasterin and lullyin for lenders miraben, sa's seer-dush, avree a boro hev. An' when len san sar jalled lug, the Rommany chals welled adoi an' latched adusta bitti barrels o' tatto-panni, an' fino covvas, for dovo mushis were 'mugglers, and the Roms lelled sar they mukked pali. An' dovo sus a boro covva for the Rommany chals, an' they pii'd sar graias, an' the raklis an' juvas jalled in kushni heezis for booti divvuses. An' dovo sus kerro pash Bo-Peep--a boro puvius adree bori chumures, pash Hastings in Sussex.

When 'mugglers nasher an' Rommany chals latch, there's kek worser cammoben for it.

TRANSLATION.

Once almost a hundred years now, when my father was a boy, one night many Gipsies were going together near the sea, when all at once the horses began whinnying and kicking and neighing, and making a great noise, and the Gipsies heard a crying out, and saw men running and rushing as if in alarm, from a great cave. And when they were all gone away together, the Gipsies went there and found many little barrels of brandy, and valuables, for those men were smugglers, and the Gipsies took all they left behind. And that was a great thing for the Gipsies, and they drank like horses, and the girls and women went in silk clothes for many days. And that was done near Bo-Peep, a great field in the hills, by Hastings in Sussex.

When smugglers lose and Gipsies find, nobody is the worse for it.

NOTES:

{0a} The reason why Gipsy words have been kept unchanged was fully illustrated one day in a Gipsy camp in my hearing, when one man declaring of a certain word that it was only **kennick** or slang, and not "Rommanis," added, "It can't be Rommanis, because everybody knows it. When a word gets to be known to everybody, it's no longer Rommanis."

{1} Lavengro and the Rommany Rye: London, John Murray.

{5} To these I would add "Zelda's Fortune," now publishing in the **Cornhill Magazine**.

{21} Educated Chinese often exercise themselves in what they call "handsome talkee," or "talkee leeson" (i.e., reason), by sitting down and uttering, by way of assertion and rejoinder, all the learned and wise sentences which they can recall. In their conversation and on their crockery, before every house and behind every counter, the elegant formula makes its appearance, teaching people not merely **how** to think, but what should be thought, and when.

{24} Probably from the modern Greek [Greek text], the sole of the foot, **i.e**., a track. Panth, a road, Hindustani.

{26} Pott: "Die Zigeuner in Europa and Asien," vol. ii, p. 293.

{30} Two hundred (shel) years growing, two hundred years losing his coat, two hundred years before he dies, and then he loses all his blood and is no longer good.

{32} The words of the Gipsy, as I took them down from his own lips, were as follows:--

"Bawris are kushto habben. You can latcher adusta 'pre the bors. When they're pirraben pauli the puvius, or tale the koshters, they're kek kushti habben. The kushtiest are sovven sar the wen. Lel'em and tove 'em and chiv 'em adree the kavi, with panny an' a bitti lun. The simmun's kushto for the yellow jaundice."

I would remind the reader that in ***every instance*** where the original Gipsy language is given, it was written down or ***noted*** during conversation, and subsequently written out and read to a Gipsy, by whom it was corrected. And I again beg the reader to remember, that every Rommany phrase is followed by a translation into English.

{33} Dr Pott intimates that ***scharos***, a globe, may be identical with ***sherro***, a head. When we find, however, that in German Rommany ***tscharo*** means goblet, pitcher, vessel, and in fact cup, it seems as if the Gipsy had hit upon the correct derivation.

{34} "Dovos yect o' the covvos that saw foki jins. When you lel a wart 'pre tutes wasters you jal 'pre the drum or 'dree the puvius till you latcher a kaulo bawris--yeck o' the boro kind with kek ker apre him, an' del it apre the caro of a kaulo kosh in the bor, and ear the bawris mullers, yeck divvus pauli the waver for shtar or pange divvuses the wart'll kinner away-us. 'Dusta chairusses I've pukkered dovo to Gorgios, an' Gorgios have kaired it, an' the warts have yuzhered avree their wasters."

{35} Among certain tribes in North America, tobacco is both burned before and smoked "unto" the Great Spirit.

{38} This word palindrome, though Greek, is intelligible to every Gipsy. In both languages it means "back on the road."

{53} The Krallis's Gav, King's Village, a term also applied to Windsor.

{65} Pronounced cuv-vas, like ***covers*** without the ***r***.

{70} The Lord's Prayer in pure English Gipsy:--

"Moro Dad, savo djives oteh drey o charos, te caumen Gorgio ta Rommanny chal tiro nav, te awel tiro tem, te kairen tiro lav aukko prey puv, sar kairdios oteh drey o charos. Dey men todivvus more divvuskoe moro, ta for dey men pazorrhus tukey sar men for-denna len pazhorrus amande; ma muck te petrenna drey caik temptaciones; ley men abri sor doschder. Tiro se o tem, mi-duvel, tiro o zoozlu vast, tiro sor koskopen drey sor cheros. Avali. Tachipen."

Specimens of old English Gipsy, preserving grammatical forms, may be found in Bright's Hungary (Appendix). London, 1818. I call attention to the fact that all the specimens of the language which I give in this book simply represent ***the mod-***

ern and greatly corrupted Rommany of the roads, which has, however, assumed a peculiar form of its own.

{75} In gipsy *chores* would mean swindles. In America it is applied to small jobs.

{81} Vide chapter x.

{83} This should be **Bengo-tem** or devil land, but the Gipsy who gave me the word declared it was **bongo**.

{110} In English: "Water is the Great God, and it is Bishnoo or Vishnoo because it falls from God. *Vishnu is then the Great God*?" "Yes; there can be no forced meaning there, can there, sir? Duvel (God) is Duvel all the world over; but correctly speaking, Vishnu is God's blood--I have heard that many times. And the snow is feathers that fall from the angels' wings. And what I said, that Bishnoo is God's Blood is old Gipsy, and known by all our people."

{112} "Simurgh--a fabulous bird, *a griffin*."--*Brice's Hindustani Dictionary*.

{124} Romi in Coptic signifies *a man*.

{127} Since writing the above I have been told that among many Hindus "(good) evening" is the common greeting at any time of the day. And more recently still, meeting a gentleman who during twelve years in India had paid especial attention to all the dialects, I greeted him, as an experiment, with "Sarisham!" He replied, 'Why, that's more elegant than common Hindu--it's Persian!" "Sarisham" is, in fact, still in use in India, as among the Gipsies. And as the latter often corrupt it into *sha'shan*, so the vulgar Hindus call it "shan!" Sarishan means in Gipsy, "How are you?" but its affinity with *sarisham* is evident.

{133} Miklosich ("Uber die Mundarten de der Zigeuner," Wien, 1872) gives, it is true, 647 Rommany words of Slavonic origin, but many of these are also Hindustani. Moreover, Dr Miklosich treats as Gipsy words numbers of Slavonian words which Gipsies in Slavonian lands have Rommanised, but which are not generally Gipsy.

{171} Fortune-telling.

{189} In Egypt, as in Syria, every child is more or less marked by tattooing. Infants of the first families, even among Christians, are thus stamped.

{206} The Royston rook or crow has a greyish-white back, but is with this exception entirely black.

{209} The peacock and turkey are called lady-birds in Rommany, because, as a Gipsy told me, "they spread out their clothes, and hold up their heads and look fine, and walk proud, like great ladies." I have heard a swan called a pauno rani chillico- -a white lady-bird.

{210} To make skewers is a common employment among the poorer English Gipsies.

{213} This rhyme and metre (such as they are) were purely accidental with my narrator; but as they occurred **verb. et lit**., I set them down.

{218} This story is well known to most "travellers." It is also true, the "hero" being a **pash-and-pash**, or half-blood Rommany chal, whose name was told to me.

{219} The reader will find in Lord Lytton's "Harold" mention of an Anglo- Sax-on superstition very similar to that embodied in the story of the Seven Whistlers. This story is, however, entirely Gipsy.

{221a} This, which is a common story among the English Gipsies, and told exactly in the words here given, is implicitly believed in by them. Unfortunately, the terrible legends, but too well authenticated, of the persecutions to which their ancestors were subjected, render it very probable that it may have occurred as narrated. When Gipsies were hung and transported merely for **being** Gipsies, it is not unlikely that a persecution to death may have originated in even such a trifle as the alleged theft of a dish-clout.

{221b} Although they bear it with remarkable **apparent** indifference, Gipsies are in reality extremely susceptible to being looked at or laughed at.

{235} This story was told me in a Gipsy tent near Brighton, and afterwards repeated by one of the auditors while I transcribed it.

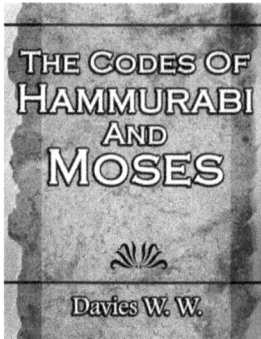

The Codes Of Hammurabi And Moses
W. W. Davies

QTY

The discovery of the Hammurabi Code is one of the greatest achievements of archaeology, and is of paramount interest, not only to the student of the Bible, but also to all those interested in ancient history...

Religion   ISBN: *1-59462-338-4*   **Pages:132**
MSRP $12.95

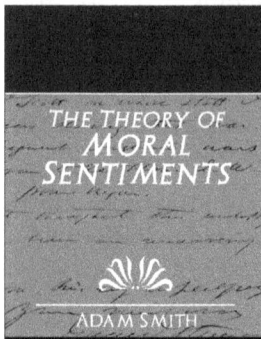

The Theory of Moral Sentiments
Adam Smith

QTY

This work from 1749. contains original theories of conscience amd moral judgment and it is the foundation for systemof morals.

Philosophy   ISBN: *1-59462-777-0*   **Pages:536**
MSRP $19.95

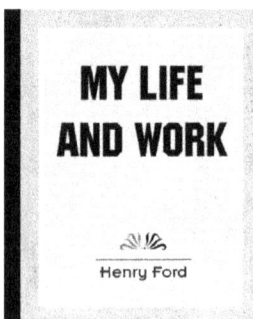

Jessica's First Prayer
Hesba Stretton

QTY

In a screened and secluded corner of one of the many railway-bridges which span the streets of London there could be seen a few years ago, from five o'clock every morning until half past eight, a tidily set-out coffee-stall, consisting of a trestle and board, upon which stood two large tin cans, with a small fire of charcoal burning under each so as to keep the coffee boiling during the early hours of the morning when the work-people were thronging into the city on their way to their daily toil...

Pages:84

Childrens   ISBN: *1-59462-373-2*   *MSRP $9.95*

My Life and Work
Henry Ford

QTY

Henry Ford revolutionized the world with his implementation of mass production for the Model T automobile. Gain valuable business insight into his life and work with his own auto-biography... "We have only started on our development of our country we have not as yet, with all our talk of wonderful progress, done more than scratch the surface. The progress has been wonderful enough but..."

Pages:300

Biographies/   ISBN: *1-59462-198-5*   *MSRP $21.95*

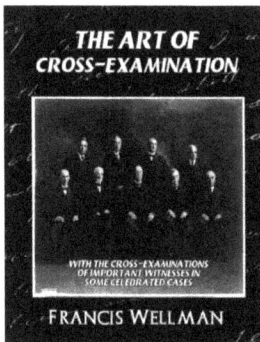

The Art of Cross-Examination
Francis Wellman

QTY

I presume it is the experience of every author, after his first book is published upon an important subject, to be almost overwhelmed with a wealth of ideas and illustrations which could readily have been included in his book, and which to his own mind, at least, seem to make a second edition inevitable. Such certainly was the case with me; and when the first edition had reached its sixth impression in five months, I rejoiced to learn that it seemed to my publishers that the book had met with a sufficiently favorable reception to justify a second and considerably enlarged edition. ..

Reference   ISBN: *1-59462-647-2*

Pages:412
MSRP $19.95

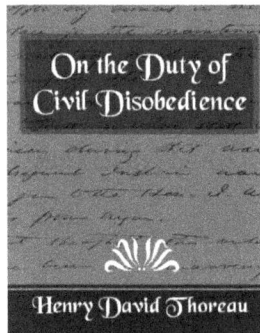

On the Duty of Civil Disobedience
Henry David Thoreau

QTY

Thoreau wrote his famous essay, On the Duty of Civil Disobedience, as a protest against an unjust but popular war and the immoral but popular institution of slave-owning. He did more than write—he declined to pay his taxes, and was hauled off to gaol in consequence. Who can say how much this refusal of his hastened the end of the war and of slavery ?

Law   ISBN: *1-59462-747-9*

Pages:48
MSRP $7.45

Dream Psychology Psychoanalysis for Beginners
Sigmund Freud

QTY

Sigmund Freud, born Sigismund Schlomo Freud (May 6, 1856 - September 23, 1939), was a Jewish-Austrian neurologist and psychiatrist who co-founded the psychoanalytic school of psychology. Freud is best known for his theories of the unconscious mind, especially involving the mechanism of repression; his redefinition of sexual desire as mobile and directed towards a wide variety of objects; and his therapeutic techniques, especially his understanding of transference in the therapeutic relationship and the presumed value of dreams as sources of insight into unconscious desires.

Psychology   ISBN: *1-59462-905-6*

Pages:196
MSRP $15.45

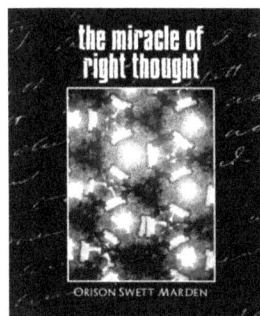

The Miracle of Right Thought
Orison Swett Marden

QTY

Believe with all of your heart that you will do what you were made to do. When the mind has once formed the habit of holding cheerful, happy, prosperous pictures, it will not be easy to form the opposite habit. It does not matter how improbable or how far away this realization may see, or how dark the prospects may be, if we visualize them as best we can, as vividly as possible, hold tenaciously to them and vigorously struggle to attain them, they will gradually become actualized, realized in the life. But a desire, a longing without endeavor, a yearning abandoned or held indifferently will vanish without realization.

Self Help   ISBN: *1-59462-644-8*

Pages:360
MSRP $25.45

QTY

☐ **The Rosicrucian Cosmo-Conception Mystic Christianity** by *Max Heindel*   ISBN: *1-59462-188-8* **$38.95**
The Rosicrucian Cosmo-conception is not dogmatic, neither does it appeal to any other authority than the reason of the student. It is: not controversial, but is: sent forth in the, hope that it may help to clear...   New Age/Religion Pages 646

☐ **Abandonment To Divine Providence** by *Jean-Pierre de Caussade*   ISBN: *1-59462-228-0* **$25.95**
"The Rev. Jean Pierre de Caussade was one of the most remarkable spiritual writers of the Society of Jesus in France in the 18th Century. His death took place at Toulouse in 1751. His works have gone through many editions and have been republished...   Inspirational/Religion Pages 400

☐ **Mental Chemistry** by *Charles Haanel*   ISBN: *1-59462-192-6* **$23.95**
Mental Chemistry allows the change of material conditions by combining and appropriately utilizing the power of the mind. Much like applied chemistry creates something new and unique out of careful combinations of chemicals the mastery of mental chemistry...   New Age Pages 354

☐ **The Letters of Robert Browning and Elizabeth Barret Barrett 1845-1846 vol II**   ISBN: *1-59462-193-4* **$35.95**
by *Robert Browning* and *Elizabeth Barrett*   Biographies Pages 596

☐ **Gleanings In Genesis (volume I)** by *Arthur W. Pink*   ISBN: *1-59462-130-6* **$27.45**
Appropriately has Genesis been termed "the seed plot of the Bible" for in it we have, in germ form, almost all of the great doctrines which are afterwards fully developed in the books of Scripture which follow...   Religion/Inspirational Pages 420

☐ **The Master Key** by *L. W. de Laurence*   ISBN: *1-59462-001-6* **$30.95**
In no branch of human knowledge has there been a more lively increase of the spirit of research during the past few years than in the study of Psychology, Concentration and Mental Discipline. The requests for authentic lessons in Thought Control, Mental Discipline and...   New Age/Business Pages 422

☐ **The Lesser Key Of Solomon Goetia** by *L. W. de Laurence*   ISBN: *1-59462-092-X* **$9.95**
This translation of the first book of the "Lernegton" which is now for the first time made accessible to students of Talismanic Magic was done, after careful collation and edition, from numerous Ancient Manuscripts in Hebrew, Latin, and French...   New Age/Occult Pages 92

☐ **Rubaiyat Of Omar Khayyam** by *Edward Fitzgerald*   ISBN:*1-59462-332-5* **$13.95**
Edward Fitzgerald, whom the world has already learned, in spite of his own efforts to remain within the shadow of anonymity, to look upon as one of the rarest poets of the century, was born at Bredfield, in Suffolk, on the 31st of March, 1809. He was the third son of John Purcell...   Music Pages 172

☐ **Ancient Law** by *Henry Maine*   ISBN: *1-59462-128-4* **$29.95**
The chief object of the following pages is to indicate some of the earliest ideas of mankind, as they are reflected in Ancient Law, and to point out the relation of those ideas to modern thought.   Religion/History Pages 452

☐ **Far-Away Stories** by *William J. Locke*   ISBN: *1-59462-129-2* **$19.45**
"Good wine needs no bush, but a collection of mixed vintages does. And this book is just such a collection. Some of the stories I do not want to remain buried for ever in the museum files of dead magazine-numbers an author's not unpardonable vanity..."   Fiction Pages 272

☐ **Life of David Crockett** by *David Crockett*   ISBN: *1-59462-250-7* **$27.45**
"Colonel David Crockett was one of the most remarkable men of the times in which he lived. Born in humble life, but gifted with a strong will, an indomitable courage, and unremitting perseverance...   Biographies/New Age Pages 424

☐ **Lip-Reading** by *Edward Nitchie*   ISBN: *1-59462-206-X* **$25.95**
Edward B. Nitchie, founder of the New York School for the Hard of Hearing, now the Nitchie School of Lip-Reading, Inc, wrote "LIP-READING Principles and Practice". The development and perfecting of this meritorious work on lip-reading was an undertaking...   How-to Pages 400

☐ **A Handbook of Suggestive Therapeutics, Applied Hypnotism, Psychic Science**   ISBN: *1-59462-214-0* **$24.95**
by *Henry Munro*   Health/New Age/Health/Self-help Pages 376

☐ **A Doll's House: and Two Other Plays** by *Henrik Ibsen*   ISBN: *1-59462-112-8* **$19.95**
Henrik Ibsen created this classic when in revolutionary 1848 Rome. Introducing some striking concepts in playwriting for the realist genre, this play has been studied the world over.   Fiction/Classics/Plays 308

☐ **The Light of Asia** by *sir Edwin Arnold*   ISBN: *1-59462-204-3* **$13.95**
In this poetic masterpiece, Edwin Arnold describes the life and teachings of Buddha. The man who was to become known as Buddha to the world was born as Prince Gautama of India but he rejected the worldly riches and abandoned the reigns of power when...   Religion/History/Biographies Pages 170

☐ **The Complete Works of Guy de Maupassant** by *Guy de Maupassant*   ISBN: *1-59462-157-8* **$16.95**
"For days and days, nights and nights, I had dreamed of that first kiss which was to consecrate our engagement, and I knew not on what spot I should put my lips..."   Fiction/Classics Pages 240

☐ **The Art of Cross-Examination** by *Francis L. Wellman*   ISBN: *1-59462-309-0* **$26.95**
Written by a renowned trial lawyer, Wellman imparts his experience and uses case studies to explain how to use psychology to extract desired information through questioning.   How-to/Science/Reference Pages 408

☐ **Answered or Unanswered?** by *Louisa Vaughan*   ISBN: *1-59462-248-5* **$10.95**
Miracles of Faith in China   Religion Pages 112

☐ **The Edinburgh Lectures on Mental Science (1909)** by *Thomas*   ISBN: *1-59462-008-3* **$11.95**
This book contains the substance of a course of lectures recently given by the writer in the Queen Street Hall, Edinburgh. Its purpose is to indicate the Natural Principles governing the relation between Mental Action and Material Conditions...   New Age/Psychology Pages 148

☐ **Ayesha** by *H. Rider Haggard*   ISBN: *1-59462-301-5* **$24.95**
Verily and indeed it is the unexpected that happens! Probably if there was one person upon the earth from whom the Editor of this, and of a certain previous history, did not expect to hear again...   Classics Pages 380

☐ **Ayala's Angel** by *Anthony Trollope*   ISBN: *1-59462-352-X* **$29.95**
The two girls were both pretty, but Lucy who was twenty-one who supposed to be simple and comparatively unattractive, whereas Ayala was credited, as her Bombwhat romantic name might show, with poetic charm and a taste for romance. Ayala when her father died was nineteen...   Fiction Pages 484

☐ **The American Commonwealth** by *James Bryce*   ISBN: *1-59462-286-8* **$34.45**
An interpretation of American democratic political theory. It examines political mechanics and society from the perspective of Scotsman James Bryce   Politics Pages 572

☐ **Stories of the Pilgrims** by *Margaret P. Pumphrey*   ISBN: *1-59462-116-0* **$17.95**
This book explores pilgrims religious oppression in England as well as their escape to Holland and eventual crossing to America on the Mayflower, and their early days in New England...   History Pages 268

www.bookjungle.com *email: sales@bookjungle.com fax: 630-214-0564 mail: Book Jungle PO Box 2226 Champaign, IL 61825*

QTY

The Fasting Cure *by Sinclair Upton*   ISBN: *1-59462-222-1*   **$13.95**
In the Cosmopolitan Magazine for May, 1910, and in the Contemporary Review (London) for April, 1910, I published an article dealing with my experiences in fasting. I have written a great many magazine articles, but never one which attracted so much attention... New Age/Self Help/Health Pages 164

Hebrew Astrology *by Sepharial*   ISBN: *1-59462-308-2*   **$13.45**
In these days of advanced thinking it is a matter of common observation that we have left many of the old landmarks behind and that we are now pressing forward to greater heights and to a wider horizon than that which represented the mind-content of our progenitors... Astrology Pages 144

Thought Vibration or The Law of Attraction in the Thought World   ISBN: *1-59462-127-6*   **$12.95**

by William Walker Atkinson   *Psychology/Religion Pages 144*

Optimism *by Helen Keller*   ISBN: *1-59462-108-X*   **$15.95**
Helen Keller was blind, deaf, and mute since 19 months old, yet famously learned how to overcome these handicaps, communicate with the world, and spread her lectures promoting optimism. An inspiring read for everyone... Biographies/Inspirational Pages 84

Sara Crewe *by Frances Burnett*   ISBN: *1-59462-360-0*   **$9.45**
In the first place, Miss Minchin lived in London. Her home was a large, dull, tall one, in a large, dull square, where all the houses were alike, and all the sparrows were alike, and where all the door-knockers made the same heavy sound... Childrens/Classic Pages 88

The Autobiography of Benjamin Franklin *by Benjamin Franklin*   ISBN: *1-59462-135-7*   **$24.95**
The Autobiography of Benjamin Franklin has probably been more extensively read than any other American historical work, and no other book of its kind has had such ups and downs of fortune. Franklin lived for many years in England, where he was agent... Biographies/History Pages 332

Name	
Email	
Telephone	
Address	
City, State ZIP	

☐ Credit Card   ☐ Check / Money Order

Credit Card Number	
Expiration Date	
Signature	

Please Mail to: Book Jungle
PO Box 2226
Champaign, IL 61825
or Fax to: 630-214-0564

ORDERING INFORMATION

web: *www.bookjungle.com*
email: *sales@bookjungle.com*
fax: *630-214-0564*
mail: *Book Jungle PO Box 2226 Champaign, IL 61825*
or PayPal *to sales@bookjungle.com*

Please contact us for bulk discounts

DIRECT-ORDER TERMS

**20% Discount if You Order
Two or More Books**
Free Domestic Shipping!
Accepted: Master Card, Visa,
Discover, American Express

www.ingramcontent.com/pod-product-compliance
Lightning Source LLC
Chambersburg PA
CBHW081152270326
41930CB00014B/3131

* 9 7 8 1 4 3 8 5 1 7 0 7 0 *